"Mind Your Heart N
(From Death Row to 20 ʒ

Authors Note:

January 16th 2004 at approximately 1:30pm.

This was the moment that I was set free from having served over 2 decades of solitary confinement on Death Row for a crime that I had nothing to do with. I had initially been set for release at 8:am that morning, but then the authorities screwed that up big time.

I was actually driven to the last barrier of the prison and could see the smiling faces of my family outside before being told:

"Oops"! "We made a mistake",...or "not yet!" (Then they turned the van which I was seated within around and took me back to prison). All because my release paperwork was not officially stamped.

That's all of the physical set up for all this book which I needed, as I try to explain my perspectives of how it all went from that point...

Come with me mentally as I share the only personal

perspective that I actually could derive now as well, from all the many things that occurred well before that day in which I was granted my freedom.

You have to understand that I began a journey with which I really had very little control over, only to come away with a unique set of gifts in my life. Gifts that to this point, still simply astound me to realise them fully.

Anyone who has come to know my story about my disastrous childhood trauma, on through my own driven stupid self harmful lifestyle of abuse (from drinking and drugs), is probably also fully aware of how I then ended up on Death Row for crimes I had no part in.

For those of you who do not know what I went through in the lead up to my incarceration and previous life as a young person, herein is a brief...and I mean brief way to state things'

Age of 7, I get raped and had my head smashed in by a man in my area and left with brain trauma along with all the hurt of keeping it secret.

Age 17, I have been kicked out of school for being violent, addicted to booze and drugs, culminating with my attacker at now age 19, and in horrible self realizations about my own self, flee to Florida and get committed to Psychiatric hospital from mental break down from childhood PTSD.

At age 20, I was arrested for false charges of attempted murder after again back on drugs and stealing cars. That ended my life as a free person.

Thrown in jail on attempted murder of my arresting police officer who stopped me in stolen car, I made things worse for myself by making up a lie about an unsolved murder in the area. I ended up blaming a former drug companion for the deed.

The police used a jail house informant to claim that I confessed to him, the killer had the same blood type as mine, and they made the jury sickened with images of what I did not do.

I can throw in an escape from Death Row (1985), but more importantly on top of this, I offer my being the first man in history in the USA to ask for DNA testing from Death Row (1988) to prove my innocence.

All of which came to be used to free me only after a very arduous test of my humanity over many years. Somewhere within all of this initial writing to you my reader is the true journey that I made along the way.

I can still now share all of the events, offer the words of others spoken then too, as I have an unmatched recall ability from years of blank walls training my mind. It is called "Lack of new mental input", meaning you are left in a cell with all that you recall of your life playing out over and over...

Once we get past this first note about how I am sharing this, I'm just going to let you be my other side that I spoke to all along, the ID, ego, whatever one can identify as being that reflective self that you speak to?

That is who I am needing you to be for this writing.

It is my hope you can appreciate how I am offering you an "inside" to know what, and then why I ended up with

sayings like: "Harder Than Life, But Kinder Than Love".

I promise you, I think you will appreciate that effort to have to derive such things about myself when I am done writing this work about my first 20 years of freedom here.

Dedication:

I dedicate this book to everyone I ever screwed up with, to whomever I previously made feel fucked over by me, or I ruined things between us with my anger. I offer now my acknowledgment here that I have been an asshole at times, and that I have been a pain in your heart.

I have come to a point where I do not use any of this to offset the many things done to me in turn though. I just am a stand up guy in this way, as I am sharing that I get it; I can be as messed up as anyone else in the right conditions, but I try so sincerely not to fall prey to that lower self. I do so much good each chance given because I know how fucked up that I have been in my past.

Do you? Do you stick to the humble side consistently, not for those brief moments that you check yourself up? I do. I am driven to be good, be a good in someone's life, and to share good each day. That is where my head and heart are shaped in life.

I also dedicate this work and efforts to my loving mother Harriett Jayne Yarris. I got it "Sport"… I got your vision of what one can be in life, no matter what life itself does to them. You are the very reason that I am polite, kind, and loving.

Lastly, Lara Rebecca Yarris… my daughter, my dreams, my love, and all my good. This is for you honey.

CHAPTER ONE:
A WHOLE LOT
OF OTHER...

There was a whirling noise of the door to my cell being opened, and finally no one was standing before my cell with clubs and cuffs outside of my door...

You have to have balls of steel sliding your own door open for the last time. I stood tall...like I was towering above me, all the many years of bursting free sensations making me project all this energy as I walked out onto the empty dayroom in front of my cell. For 8057 days that I counted of that cell door being locked, either 23, or 24 hours per day, this was the one I waited for.

I am watching the "White Shirts" (Lieutenants and above that in rank) gathering up their nerves to come face to face with me as I walk off the cell block. I am that first guy using DNA who is proving that Death Row in Pennsylvania is really all bullshit, and that they can and did get it wrong.

My eyes lock on anyone willing to meet mine, and as it happened all that day, few held my steady gaze. I am emanating. A sense of righteous strength washed over me in my mind as I left the prison unit and out into a long hall way.

Kept thinking... I have a mindset that is now letting me sort through layers of this moment. I am a walking encyclopedia of many vast subjects... from law, to psychology, literature and the sciences. I needed every bit of it to handle this moment.

This all came to me from a notion of my dying. I waited years for my execution while trying to learn how to become as beautifully alive at the moment of death as I could imagine myself being. And that was then reflected in my daily precise mannerisms which guided me along.

I was at the height of my beauty against the near utter destruction of me on Death Row due to serious medical issues complicating it all on top of this.

At that moment of release I had just battled 2 years of near death illness of Hepatitis-C. (Blood poisoning brought on by dental treatment in prison). I was driven so deep and dark from this suffering that I asked to be executed, rather than die of impacted bowl syndrome that this illness causes.

Thinking then how I was told that I needed to have a liver transplant by the prison staff, I knew partly why the state gave up and let me go now. It was how they knew that I had only a few years to live upon release was my prognosis (unless I got another person to die and get their Liver).

So, a year after DNA results, I was set free...

I knew all of this as I passed by the cells of men who were now yelling out their final farewells to me. It was the sadly sweet way men act who literally butchered others, yet they felt a bond enough with me to sent me off with love. That was some thing not of this outside world to understand.

Oh how I felt others all flinch or come close to me as if they were drawn to my energy as I passed through the last gates leading to the outside world. I was surrounded by a team of administrators who dare not touch me, like I had something scary about me. But not one officer had a club, it was odd how they left them behind. No black tape hiding names today either. Little things...always little things cling to my mind.

I said nothing as they processed me out past the control booth. I saw my mother Jayne trying to fight through guards to get to me through thick glass walls that were just beyond me. I saw my father Mike trying hard to fight off tears...that was something I never saw in his eyes my whole life.

I got fucking pissed off thinking what they had done to my folks for years for a second. I let it burn for a bit before I gathered myself together and got my my pulse lowered. Then I walked out of the prison and up to the press with my knowing that I was about to pull off the most suave shit that these yahoos had ever seen.

First, I had to let my mother do a full on hug with me, tears of utter relief streamed down her face as she lept into my arms! That made me terrified and boldly alive.

I was hit hard by her energy and the emotions pouring out when my mother hugged me. It was from the notion that she finally came and got her son home were all I felt beaming into me. I tasted her tears when I kissed her face, I was not letting myself cry though. I had no need to.

I had waited for 23 years for this moment, I just had to hug my father next, feel his bones through his clothes like never before. Get through that and I can be man enough to pull things back from the brink.

Gone was the muscled frame of Mike Yarris as I embraced him, now entering his 70's the many years of life my father knew were hard. I knew what I had to do for him to feel strong. I knew he needed a spark mentally, so I whispered into his ear how we should get the fuck out of there before they change their minds again.

That seemed to work well, as my father laughed as emotionally strained of a laugh as anyone could who was now letting out that breath which you thought was never getting out of your chest.

Emboldened by this interaction with my parents, I then walked up to the cameras and microphones of the press who were assembled outside of the prison front doors. I did not say one word about what was done to me and mine. I knew that I put my own self on death row as much as they did. And because of that point, I was not going to join in that same lame parade of who said what, nor what they became from their lies.

No, I began asking for help for men behind me in the prison that I stood before.

I did the only decent thing which I could come up with so that no hate got aimed at me. Oh no sir, I was keeping my head down and was being humble all day, was my attitude.

Then, as I finished speaking to the press and began to walk towards the visitor's parking area of the prison, I saw my ex wife Jacque standing by her car. I hated me having to live this anti-climatic moment right then.

I hated looking at her 15 years after I had told her that DNA would set me free.

Even more it burned me mentally for how I told her that I was in love with her as she sat in a maximum security level prison visiting room behind glass. The fact that she left me there to die 7 years before that day I saw her again was not hurting me, I just felt sad for a dream that died between us.

I wanted to step back for a minute and not have to deal with this shit, but there I was, all hugs and embraces to the third person that day. I let a woman I was truly in love with hold me and I felt and smelled her female warmth, so I was on the verge of puking. Yeah fuck it, here is the truth of why holding me was making me so messed up.

I went from November of 1989 until december of 2003 without a human hand ever touching me.

THAT fucked with my head at times, as it also taught me things that no one could get their minds around, without a similar time spent in such a manner as mine was.

Hell, few will even grasp how I can absorb energy from touch like its a drug, (or a delicious drink that you never stop wanting) is what I expect, but I will try my best to prove how it is a real "thing" to me from being starved of touch for 15 years...

I am serious. I have a knowledge of a magic that is real. I can hold someone and I feel molecule level connections, as I then absorb their touch with thirst like no other.

Which all really sucked at first when I just got set free from my cell that day. I was about to go from no human hands touching me, to dozens of hugs, touches and

embraces from family all at once.

I was so glad we all hurriedly got into cars and drove a short way to a restaurant, hoping to settle everyone's nerves and try to eat. We had to soon drive over 300 miles with my parents to their home in Philadelphia with my friend Pan Tucker driving them on behalf of the Federal Defender's office in Philadelpia facing us that day.

First though, I was watching the world outside of the car which Jaque drove me away from the prison inside of without metal cages and chains on my body. Never thought I would be alive out here is all I kept thinking as we left the grounds heading towards Pittsburgh.

As Jaque drove, I thought about how I met her...

When we met she was a volunteer for a prison rights advocacy group, while working in the mental health field for abused children as well. Jacque was like some dream coming into a jail and then falling in love with me.

I was 27 years old, I had a combined 105 years of sentences and was sentenced to die. I had met Jacque only due to interviews being conducted by Pam Tucker and Jaque to garner evidence of abuse to get the prison unit where I was housed in shut down. (It finally was shut by court order in 1995 thanks to their work)

Attractive, well educated and 32 years old, why on earth would such a woman fall in love with a man losing his hair badly, wearing prison issued eye glasses, and had extensive abuse done to him physically for his escaping from prison? I knew her reasons were born of dreams of romantic life after all this dreams..., but to anyone else who did not understand why she married me while I wore handcuffs (and stuck by me for 9 years), they could only think she was a fool for having done that.

Here it was over 16 years later from when I met her in 1987-88, to looking at her in profile as she drove the car. I had no emotions as I told her how lame it was to have my release botched earlier, and how this whole thing just dragged out. I did not do any visits back down memory lane with her, she deserved to be spared that. When we got to the place we agreed to meet for lunch, I was actually glad that I was able to leave it all on a neutral note with my now ex-wife. I was going to be dealing with too much here and now to revisit any yesterdays with anyone.

I was also trying to keep anyone around me at that luncheon from knowing how I really could not grasp how they looked. One or two visits a year, some photos, that stuff does not make what aging does to people a reality.

I don't want to look at how shrunken looking now that my parents are as they sit across from me at the Diner we were now inside of.

I don't even want to talk to them about the car ride I just shared with my ex-wife that was no one's business, as it was awkwardly beautiful.

Meanwhile "Poppy", as everyone called my dad,
is so upset and wrung through. I can see the weariness on his face as he had endured my release being delayed over a week to that point.

All of this while my older brother Mikey was in a hospital at that moment, they told me that as an aside conversation while they ate... Mikey, having been run over by a car across from their home just three days before this meal was in a bad condition I was told flatly.

As I looked at Poppy sitting there before me. I felt my heart sink for how my little brother had died of a drug overdose in his basement in 2002, and how he came down in the morning to find him sitting on the sofa down there, dead at age 39...that was only 2 years before that moment in which I sat before my father.

I went back mentally to that time... How hard it was for me to try to call home from Death Row to comfort my parents as they lost their youngest child. Then it hit me how it was so brutal how my sister Anna Marie hung up the phone on me when I made an emergency family phone call upon being told that my brother was dead. I did not even get to have a chance to speak to my mother. I ate all of that painful shit and moved on...

Anna hated me and made that shit known to me after a while, so I knew this was just her way to make me feel worthless when I was trying to speak to my parents and siblings when Marty had died. I lost my little brother same as she did, but as far as she was concerned, I was right where I belonged and "fuck you, don't call us back"...

I kept thinking of all of the things that I saw Poppy have to handle as I tried to order the only thing on the menu that I thought that I could eat...Bread.

I asked for fresh baked bread and as I did so, I told all of others at the table about a childhood memory of mine.

Mentally I had to stop myself from thinking all the bad shit that both of my parents endured by trying this then.

So, I regaled them a story about how Poppy worked two jobs when I was young. I told them how my mom and I worked out a deal.

If I gave Poppy a massage, I would get fresh rolls from his second job as a baker at night in payment.

After his first job as a roofer in the day, I would give my dad a massage as he napped, and he would bring me home a paper sack full of warm rolls that he made for me. I would be falling asleep at the dinner table in my PJs, with tomato soup in a pot on the stove, just waiting for my father to bring me my treats. "Mmmm"...,

Pumpernickel, Black Russian rolls, Sesame seed dinner rolls were all my delight. I told them how basically bread kept me going inside as well. It seemed to work and everyone began to eat. I got a few bites in and no, not today Nicky, you got way too much stomach acid going on, your left eye is throbbing...

My left eye will never be right, my face is going to crumble at some point, and I have broken bones that were never allowed any treatment all over my body. Thus initially, any food was going to be too rich for me, or just too much for me to process.

I had to get away from that table. I could not sit there with my mother, father, Pam Tucker, and my ex-wife, Jacque who were all sitting before me so able to handle such a huge event like this.

All of them being normal and eating like that was too much in the aftermath of my release. I was not cool with this, so I literally asked to go outside…and my father sensing my situation was hard on me mentally, went with me to make sure that I was okay.

Sitting there in the cold next to my father no less than two hours after being in a Maximum Security prison was like being lifted from some fog that holds your head down.

I was so tired as I hadn't been sleeping the past week much. Thinking about the next 5 hours drive in a car to Philadelphia, to what was waiting for me that night at my parents house on top of it all, really made me really uneasy.

I asked my father if he had a place for me to sleep at his house. With yet another hurt look on his face, My dad said how my oldest nephew (who was in some Federal prison then for a series of bank robberies) had his girlfriend and their son living in my parents house. This is so Philly I told myself listening to the news...

Since my brother was going to need 24 hours care when he got out of the hospital my dad told me, I was going to have only one night in my old childhood bedroom. Then I would have to sleep in the basement on a sofa-bed.

I understood. Three bedroom house and all of the three beds taken. Listening to Poppy next explain how Mikey had gotten run over and nearly killed just a couple days before this, I just hung my head. I had been the cause of so much of this man's suffering like this, I felt like whatever he needed me to do, I was going to do it with glee. Or try to.

This was as fucked a start to my life as I could imagine. I changed the mood of such somber moments with my father. I got him to laugh about the changes in life since I was locked up 23 years before that day. It was just me with silly reminders how cars no longer had hubcaps, or how money changed. The second one was a trick to get 20 dollars off my father to get him to laugh. That was all I could try, it was all too surreal otherwise.

The drive to Philadelphia began with my parents seated behind me that was facilitated by Pam Tucker driving us all. I rode shotgun up front, my father behind me on the rear passenger side, and my mother seated behind Pam. I sat half turned in my seat trying to not get motion sickness, as when you have been locked inside of a small cell for many years, you get motion sickness quickly with being placed inside of moving vehicles.

I got the radio station out of Pittsburgh that I listened to from my cell in prison tuned into on the car stereo and tried to not be overwhelmed visually by the outside.

I have a unique ability to identify with that wild animal that has been set free from a cage that we often see in film or videos. I know what that heart pounding first few moments feel like to that creature who's eyes are shocked into a giant new reality.

I had to work hard to not indulge in anything mentally, I kept being mindful that my parents were needing me to be one less fucking heartache that day. Just keep smiling Nicky, talk to them and make them see how you are still mentally okay.

I just knew that this was just a terrible start to what was going to be a brutal reality for me. Meanwhile, they all were fooled into this false sense of relief that they had gotten their son and family member back.

You see, I was riding in that car knowing that my life just eneded. The life, the man whom I became in that life, and all the many beautiful developments had just died when I had to go away from that sobriety driven elevation. I was leaving school to go try and now be a grown up.

I had studied 6 years of psychology courses via the Pell grant system while in prison. I had a very deft (and personal) understanding of dysfunction, developmental issues, or family dynamic break-downs that are all due to the spiraling substance abuse issues that my family had.

I knew that numerous members of my family were

functioning alcoholics or drug abusers . I had 23 years of

phone calls and letters from my mother to tell me all of the sad parade that I was on the sidelines of being part of.

It was half way along the car journey to my parents when we stopped for fuel and toilets. My mother was on the mobile phone that she owned, talking to my sister Anna. She was listening more than speaking, and I knew this was a tough call for her to deal with as I stood next to her at the rest area.

My mom was doing her best to make that appeasing effort to handle information she was meant to relate to me as she hung up the phone. I got my game face on and waited.

This was like my mother's first wish that her family, that was so torn asunder from so much pain, now could

start to heal, finally…

Fuck. This was really not fair. I gave no fucks if Anna was there, but this was some huge thing that they were expecting a huge blow up over because of the funeral phone call. This was me coming back from the grave after someone kicked me while I was in a cell. Anna and others in my family all blame Marty becoming a crack head (and or alcoholic who used to rob my parents home so much that they had to deadbolt their doors) on how I bullied Marty as a boy.

Yep, that is what they came to use to offset all of them watching a grown adult ruin his life with any drugs he could use. The other 80 per cent of my family who did drugs or drank said it was his sadness for my going to Death Row made him kill himself. Basically Marty only died because of what I did to this family.

I am not making this up as I was told all of this in the years that had gone on and on with my kin.

At some point Anna went from coming and visiting me inside of Graterford Prison in 1982, to "I fucking hate you for what you did to our family" some years later.

I swear to God, Anna was cool with me, still loved me and came to see me in prison at first like I said, but then she hated me all of a sudden. I learned it was because she was being clubbed with me as the main reason she was to suffer, so she was embarrassed by me... This is the reaction others have when they fell an embarrassment from your bond to them. Mainly she held onto the "Me" as to whom I was before I went to jail as a driving force of this. She clung to hate of that kid whom I was is what this was all driven by. Complex way here to simply say how Anna hated the junky and thief that I was, so she was not going to let my past ever be forgotten by me.

It would not matter what I went through inside of jail to pay for being that screwed up kid, she was going to just make sure I felt her scorn from outside.

That was how Anna treated me before that phone call that day I was set free, the one who heard it was me who was calling home during my brother Marty's funeral in 2002 and then rudely hung the phone up on me.

I could have indulged my slight from back then and broke my mother's heart in my first hours out of jail. I was not going to do that to her, or to myself actually. This had to be my first learning experience of how to handle people who were going to see me as they once knew me. Do you see about how fucking bright that I needed to be to mentally handle just this pre-entrance to my new life in that car journey? Wish to God it was not really what all went down for me.

I told my mother to tell Anna that she could be there when we all got to Philadelphia. I did not want to talk to her though, that direct dip back into how delicate this minefield was going to be was too much then. I felt this omnipresent and negative cloud over me was enough right then to wake me up to where I was going and who was there to meet. Get yourself together Nicky, ask yourself what is this going to be? That is what I went to work on while we drove again.

I knew a few hours later what this all was going to be when we pulled behind my parents house to be hastily be given a Philadelphia Eagles cap to replace my prison issue baseball cap. We had family members hiding on the side street do this quick swap, so I could then pretend I just got there for the press out front to see me wearing the team hat. Why?

The team was chasing a championship that year and they were hoping how I would be given free tickets to the playoff game, or even bigger…superbowl tickets for pity!

It was next all followed by my being interviewed standing in front of my parents house "ensemble" fashion, with my siblings cutting off the interview when they felt like I had spoken too long solo to the press. Calling for an end of the Death Penalty in Pennsylvania was not appealing.

I swear, I felt inside as if I was not out there as the man who just got set free from Death Row, I was in the now projected control of my family who had this very staged setting moment with me so, we can get football tickets.

Of course I did not get tickets to anything for fuck's sake.

Then came the moment of me walking inside, and everyone is downstairs in the living room. Family. Some I know, and some I just saw for the first time outside of photographic images. I smile hopefully.

Then, as if on cue, a moment they were all waiting for next came without any words. When the whole room knows a moment is coming, you can feel it from them. This was that moment we all get...

They all were primed for this event where they knew Anna was upstairs alone waiting for me to get done being interviewed, and how she was waiting upstairs until I came inside so she could come down the steps like this big encounter.

Like a scene from some deeply flawed film, she then walked down the steps only half way, and everyone was watching us each for what would happen next... They all knew what she did to me when Marty died. This was like a measuring stick for them all. This would show them as to how I would set aside deliberate cruel acts done to me by any of them in the past.

I at least took control then, as I walked up the steps so that whatever rehearsed performance that I was about to deal with from Anna was not done to me in front of a room full of others to witness.

We went into the back bedroom where I had one night of sleep waiting for me. Anna stood in front of a big set of dresser drawers that had a mirror on the wall behind it. I stood looking at her in half profile. On death Row I had learned that when you enter a situation, say nothing as much as possible.

You learn so much letting the other person search for validations to what they say more often than not. I just waited for what she had in mind, and then I would set things in motion from there. I am not stupid, I spent the rest of that car ride waiting for this shit, I was on my game. I am not some junkie asshole loser, some day when you read here what I now write Anna, you will see how I saved my best for now.

With a big long release of breath, a sigh at the end of it as she let go of some look of a big decision that she was just then making...Anna then told me how she was aware that everyone down stairs was now thinking that we were up here soothing our past squabbles out, but that really for her, she had been hating me for so long that she wasn't sure she could stop now.

I looked at her a long moment when she finished, long enough to do a quick ascertainment of her level of life development. I put that against whatever she could ever contrive of the absolute shit that I was just put through in prison... and then I dismissed her right then and there.

I would invest no feelings for this person standing now before me because I learned to do that as well on Death Row.

I dismissed any feelings for her, any want to love her again, as I then let go of any feeling that she was my sister any more than some stranger was to me on the streets.

Literally I thanked her, and then I told her then that I respected her for openly telling me to my face that she hated me. I was not looking for an apology and she was not offering any.

I told Anna how I was going downstairs and how I was going to help her pull off this charade of us making things all appear to be better between us. You know, for the rest of my family to all be happy. I said it with total chagrin, as well. I was like, that's how you want to play this shit, then fine by me lady. I just got more shit than you to deal with today.

Anna wasn't aware of how many people whom I had dealt with inside of jail who had to have a facade like this between us for the rest to believe about about them and I, even if it was all just bullshit.

I will say this again, I have a weird gift of absorbing energy from others. Anna made hers known to me right off as being this harsh and cold one humans can actually project. I felt relief for being so twigged in like this on picking things up right away. I told myself going back down to the living room, if I pay attention to their energy how I might be able to protect myself...

That first night though, it was too much too soon to hug anyone after a short while of having so much human varitations of energy touching me mentally like this with one with Anna, or physically just being held.

The jovial energy with booze, and having all the many personalities in my family on display was near to being way too much at times that evening. I had to sincerely fight the want to get out of there when folks got all drunk and loud in front of me.

By 9:pm that night I had already rung the phone of a total stranger in New Jersey and asked if I could come there. They said no.

Lawyers could not help me, I had no friends left from childhood, I was so stressed out that yes, I literally tried to run off my first night out.

I am not fucking around with lies about this first night home being a disaster. When the news came on about 10:pm, and I had to watch what I finally looked like at the age of 42 on a Television screen, I was dealing with real heartache and sorrow. It felt like I had just gotten stripped naked and shown to be a pathetic refugee from my own life. I did not have a mirror in my cell, I did not know what I looked like literally, so what a crazy mind blowing moment for me to deal with.

I started to internalize over all this when the news clips stopped. We were all sitting at a long dining room table, as I told my father that I was not sure if I could deal with my lawyers wanting me to do a presser. I said how they wanted me to stand in front of 23 boxes of legal work that my case had accumulated in their offices the following Monday for impactful images when I spoke.

I felt so ashamed that I had lost my hair, was wearing prison issued eye glasses, all while I was down under 200 lbs. for the first time since the age of 20.

I had sallow skin form lack of sunlight for decades and medical toxins made me look jaundiced. I asked my father if I should wear a hat with a suit and try to look presentable that way If I did do the press event.

That was the moment my sister Anna decided to no longer hold back her feelings, and with my mother by then blessedly in her bed asleep, she launched on me.

Anna told me what a "dickhead" that I was going to look like if I wore a baseball cap with a nice suit at the press conference.

I was so stung that this was her issue, how I might now embarrass her family with my appearance, that I shut down. I did not have any cleverness or quips, I just looked at her with the most lost feelings for why she had to snap like this over my feeling old and ugly.

My need to defend myself was not needed by me, as right then my father shot forward in his chair and told my sister to shut her mouth.

In disbelief I watched as he shouted that I was his son, and how she was to leave me the fuck alone about how I looked. Poppy said that she had no idea what they had done to me in that hell hole I just got out of.

That moment of Poppy standing up for me broke my heart.

I was so tired of this drunken bullshit, all while everyone who was there that night told me that if I drank, that I was going to just be such a loser like I always used to be. What a joke this was all on me right then.

Oh how fucked up of a moment on my first night home that my father had to explode in horror of how I was being bullied about losing my hair, or how I looked.

I got the fuck out of there before I lost my shit. I ran down to the basement where I found myself just standing outside of the rear basement door while listening to them up above me, now discussing the aftermath of what just went down moments before.

I heard Anna leaving then, and I had to deal with one thing more than any other mentally... No blood.

Yelling like that inside of jail leads always to how blood soon follows. That is rule.

Having not been around arguing like this for years, hell I was not allowed the luxury to argue, and hearing an outburst with pitched emotions like this one made me now internalize it all.

I was freaked out from how no one bled. No violence after shouting made me shocked into an anticlimactic emptiness that then was making me feel all nauseous.

I was so urgently in need of urinating, that as I stood there peeing against the back wall, I had to lean my head on the cold wall of the house to stop all the pain that was in my head.

I had just went from a maximum security prison, straight into the most complex set of emotional upheaval anyone could have imagined. How could I not be freaked out to some degree?

I never did go upstairs and try to sleep that night in the childhood bedroom that I once shared with my two brothers. No one in my position was going to sleep that night, no way to trust this is even all real yet, was how I was approaching it things.

When everyone left my parents home I went up said goodnight to Poppy. I told him to please go sleep. What a man to handle this one day I thought. You don't say anything lame or placating to a man after a day like this I thought.

I sat down there in the basement that night watching the US and Iraq war news. I sat listening to all of the many big countries using embargo to starve the people living there until they rose up and helped America overthrow their own government. Motivational starvation.

That is what I mentally called it as that news clip played and it was just was so weirdly eerie to me why I would so focus on that...

Sitting there thinking about how Pennsylvania would feel if someone clever like me messed up all their trade for what they did to me, I smiled as I had an idea from watching this thing with Iraq.

A few hours later as I sat on the sofa in my parents basement (where my little brother died of a drugs and alcohol overdose), I came up with some next level shit to deal with my situation that was not dysfunctionally driven.

Sitting in the wreckage of my first day outside of prison, I was well beyond any bullshit anger, I was far too well advanced mentally to capitulate, and I had one need above all else: Some how, and in some way, this event had to have a meaning to me somehow.

From the moment that the courthouse was struck by lightening on the very day that I was sentenced to die in 1982, to the many times God saved me from attacks in prison, somehow this was going to hold meaningfulness for me.

In a few hours from sitting there, I would go with my mother to the hospital and go get my brother to bring him to my parents house, that was all I could think of.

But before any of that family saga, I needed some reason beyond all of this to cling to sanity.

I was informed that party night number one at my parents was to be followed by another party night. That of the rest of my family who wanted to come see me now that I was free wanted to bring some beer and food and celebrate it all. Like a celebrity, but not, I was going to meet and greet and go through the hugs and energy all over and wow....just wow.

Sleep was not my only mental challenge for me on my first night outside of prison. I kept opening the rear door and going out back and looking up at the clear night sky without a cage or bars in my way. I kept having to see that I was far away from bars, chains, or always…the memories of sounds of keys rattling as men walked.

I began trying to formulate my plan for how I was going to try not just endure handling the ravaged body from Hepatitis-C infection and what stress was doing to me. I was going to show myself once, how truly bright that I was as a man, or this will all overwhelm me. No way now that I was letting this story end with me getting drunk, tossing in the towel, and letting Philadelphia eat me alive.

All I had to do was stay sober and pray that the stress of

being set free was not too much mentally for me while in this setting.

No matter what, I had to find out what I was capable of out here in society. I swear to God, I knew who I was whilst I was inside of prison, I had no clue who I was out here though.

No matter what anyone else thought that my freedom would be in my first days home, all I can offer anyone was that is was a whole lot of "Other". Not good, not bad, just that "other" thing so much that it really was weird.

Then combine that with all of the hurts that I did not expect were to be my reality, and I hope you my reader can see how I had to make some effort in life from it all.

It is not like I got out of prison with some big ego notion about myself that sent me chasing fame. It was literally try this way of thinking, or just wither and die here as a nobody.

I was stuck in such a horrible situation personally that I had to seek some huge inspirational thing to go and try and do, okay? That is all that a kid growing up from my area could come up with when you get crushed by the justice system and everyone around you is a mess.

You fight back because you feel for all the world like some thing, or some one out here has to be worth it all.

I hope to God that I am right to believe in this way even to this point.

NICHOLAS JAMES YARRIS

CHAPTER TWO: PROMISE ME, NICKY...

When my mother awoke on my second day of freedom I went upstairs from the basement and sat with her in the front of the house. She and my father were both awake and she sat on a chair in the front conservatory of their home with her morning coffee.

Sitting under a photo of her six children on the wall behind my mother, I was attentive to her needs to know that I was okay mentally.

I told her that I slept fine when she asked. No one mentioned the huge argument at the end, so she was still oblivious to how my night ended. I told my mother that I was looking forward to go with her and collect my brother from the hospital.

My father was off getting dressed then as he had to go to work at age of 70, still doing roofing, so it was down to me to help her get Mikey home that day.

I was told that my brother's leg was severely broken and he had a full length cast on his leg. I could only imagine the state of him as no one was there to see him while I was being set free.

Just as I was mentally dealing with doing this thing at the hospital with her, my mother looked at me intently. It went on with her formulating whatever she had to say to me, so I knew her enough to let her get to the point while politely waiting.

It began with her reminiscence of events long ago and then she sincerely paused and dispensed with that line of conversation, saying: "Nicky I need you to do me a favor please"...

I watched her face, every tiny fraction, the way that I would when I saw her on visiting day, as if that might be the last time that I saw my mother. I listened then as Jayne Yarris, fine woman that she was, explained to me how I HAD to be a kind man, a polite man. She reasoned with me how doing this would be the only thing which she would ask me to do for her in payment for what the U.S. Justice did to her family.

As she spoke to me, each layer of how I could so utterly fulfill her needed promise from me, all would be my joy.

I kept thinking: That's all you want from me mom? That "it" honey?

All that you want me to do is have a sweet nature to my personality, and be polite in a humble manner so that I can show YOU respect? Such a simple thing, yet so huge in nature to her.

Oh how her words seared into my soul as I found myself kneeling before her, like a blessed warrior who has now been charged with a dutiful mission.

Of all the moments of my life, this one was so hard to handle without emotion. I was being blessed with a promise in which I had no clue how to pull it off, knowing only that I was being asked to relinquish all manner of ego driven acts. I then just had to serve her needs for me to piously always be a good man.

I vowed both aloud and to my own self, how I was going to try.

She didn't ask me not to drink, she knew that I was not going to toss her gift that I was in her eyes into the gutter like that. My mother was appealing to me to be this unique man whom she had spent so many hours talking to inside of a prison visiting room. The one who made her feel impressed by with my poise and development that she alone shared besides my ex wife Jacque.

This was so hard on me and I found myself once more trying to break the mood with something to distract my mother as she sat before me.

I asked my mother if she remembered "the poem".

She smiled in acknowledgment of our shared memory from long before, from a visit that we shared in which she asked me what I was reading lately in an off hand way…

That simple question from her back then lead to one of my fondest memories shared with my mother on a visit inside of a prison.

For one of the few times ever, like an eager little boy I was trying to show off an intellectual trick for praise from one of my parents.

I went into a long recollection of this beautiful work that I was reading at that time, and how it was about the lone surviving poem found on the interior of a wall from a people who once lived in South America.

The poem was key to a language for people who had their entire written language erased by the invading conquistadors who had taken their lands.

On the prison visit I regaled my mother first with the driven love story between the archaeologists who were driven to revive the language of these people so that those who once spoke it could reconnect to their own heritage. I told her about the plot line in the book, and then I recited the poem that was found hidden finally after years of everyone doubting them. It was this single poem which gave this couple discovering it their first idea of how beautiful that these people were in developed thought.

Kneeling now before my mother in her home I began:

"In the evening, when all the doors are shut,
  and every sound lies sleeping,
  Memories, Like quiet Visitors, Arrive".

  My mother smiled in wonderment that I could recite this poem some 15 years after I first had told her this story the first time.

  "Nicky how the hell do you remember ever single detail of every single little thing?!" Was what my mother asked, after I smilingly finished my recital.

  I told My mother the truth in that I lived so much within the many thousands of books of which I had read, that I was hardly ever away from my own beautiful world of literature to keep me alive mentally.

  So, remembering stories from books is part of how I kept sane.

  That was a hell of a moment for her to know that I was functioning well mentally with being set free.

  Furthermore, she saw that the man who had been set free was indeed the eloquent individual whom she got to witness develop over the years.

  Jayne was the only one who doggedly kept coming back to see me year in and year out. I knew right then that if she were to know me in that world, and saw me grow and rise through many days few men could handle, then now she would see that I could fulfill her task upon me with grace.

  So crazy how all of this was to propel me forward, and I would next deal with so much with a perspective that only this one morning could have produced for me.

  Like a pre-written script of which we both knew the parts were far too important to miss, we set things into motion that morning that to this day are able to send chills up my spine. All for what a gift that my life became for me on that second day that I was free.

And as you are going to see from reading on, my life is

stacked oddly so that my best moments as the one shared above, are then always met with how things go crashing side-ways into it all manner of hard events.

Like the part of the script that sucks to be you in that scene where no matter what your piousness, you get trounced. I have this happen to me so much that I get it about my life...I get one minute of joy for every dozen or more moments of hard ones that are filled with pain.

I know the ratio is different for each of us and we all pay different sets of tolls for the roads that our lives are thrust upon. I pay without gripe as I pray to God that I can still will myself to look outwards to find a good despite the price.

I would rather be that as a man mentally anyway, rather than to just drive blindly onward to a fast goal in life.

Also, I needed some boost that morning to override last night's debacle. Maybe she had to give me some way to now face being her hope that one of her sons would make good in life.

That is what it felt like prior to going to see Mikey in his hospital bed. I literally had to find myself thinking this way as we went to the hospital to stop being all anxious about how I could get him home from a wheel chair to my mother's car without hurting him.

Mikey was still unshaven, still coming out of the fog of

alcoholism too, all while high on pain medication. Mikey definitely had to be on morphine pain medication for his leg that had been broken so badly. The medication him out of it nearly, but he was coherent enough to talk to and be aware it was me.

My older bother (by only 15 months) looked like an old man to me laying there, which really stole my memories of who Mikey was from growing up with him. I was so deflated, and I hardly hid it. Mikey moaned in reaction to me as he saw this deflated look that I wore on my face. He got all down in mood and I felt really shitty inside for having slipped up like that. I walked over to his bed and I hugged him. As I held him his energy was so blue, so not right, this was sheer pain I held.

I could not believe how fragile my big brother felt in my arms. I could not get this all right in my head.

I was so angry at how the staff had left him without changing his bed pan, bedding, or even cleaned up his face from food he hallf ate and was still laying beside him on the bed sheets.

Oh man, I was so getting him out of there, and he can have my bed, and I will care for you I told myself...I got him up and into a wheel chair and we got Mikey home. Yes he cried out in pain, yes he cursed me and yes it was aweful getting his full length cast into a sports car my mother drove back then. But yeah, I got Mikey home.

He sat in the same chair that my mother sat upon that same morning while telling me who I had to become

in life. That image then was not lost on me one bit.

We set Mikey up with his leg propped up on a cushioned stool while waiting for family to come by and start the second night of partying at my parents house. It was a Saturday so everyone was off work.

I'm looking at Mikey and I cannot imagine how he has

managed to survive this ghetto that my neighborhood was turned into while I was in prison. He had been mugged and beaten numerous times over the years while drunk in the street. My mother was even robbed at gunpoint in my brother-in-law's store across the street when she worked there to have money for Christmas gifts one year.

All around the neighborhood as I looked past Mikey there were burned out cars across the street behind the gas station, debris all over the streets, and just everywhere that I looked outside was beat down looking.

I couldn't live here. I couldn't deal with all of this depressing shit where everyone is beat down and broke. This is where everyone has to own a gun to feel safe. Kept thinking how I was told that due to the damage done to my liver from my illness. I was expected to have to need a new liver within three years. I wasn't sure then if that was my blessing or another huge blow to my chances of living here.

I felt like a chump, and it sure sucked to think how I was expected to pull some miracle out of my butt and get money together to get a place on my own and go heal.

I was willing to gloss over the family dysfunctional bullshit, I was willing to deal with poverty and living off my parents until I could get a menial job, but this feeling that I was on a shortened lease sucked. I could control the booze not affecting my liver, but the stress that was all around me? I had to be somehow next level Nicky to face this type of environment.

My God Mikey I so pitied you that first day knowing inside how I would leave you here. I had to make the choice to go while knowing you wouldn't make it without me...

That was a "have to be" situation to be dealt with at some point, but right then, I felt the truth about how I could not stay there if I was to survive.

So on came the second day of partying that was minus Anna, as she stayed clear of my parents house on that second day. Other than the muted mocking of Mikey in front of me for being out of it mentally, I did my part to interact with everyone and enjoy the re-connections with people I once knew.

It was really good to see all of my family who were all of

the ones who were collateral to this event. I had to keep

being mindful of how while they all saw this balding, middle aged man in these ill fitting clothes, that this was not me be a long shot.

I don't know what or who they saw actually, I just was somehow mentally able to go back to being the me who was in solitude while in a cell. Someone strong and at peace. I could not be drawn into dealing with that huge gap of time that was stolen from my life right then.

I was okay being this man over here, the one who can derive the perspective to have a stand alone mindset to manage what would otherwise cause serious damage to the average person.

Seriously, when I hear about others speak about their family, and what harmful dealings that they have had to endure, I always reflect back on a knowing that I have about it all.

My personal views are my own, but I came to the "Nah, fuck that" moment while mentally standing before a table that was piled high with family issues. I passed on the whole menu which was filled with how family can be a word used to excuse all manner of tired and nasty behavior.

I was shown in real time upon release that the ones bonded to you by genetics are often the ones who are entitlement driven to then fuck your head up in ways that a stranger would never have the courage to try.

I was being given not only a real time example of a lesson about family dysfunction, I was also being next presented with a choice about how I was going to live my life different from this. I guess once again right off I had to be taught all of this, right?

I asked of my self why, why did this have to be so shit like this? I thought at first it was because of all the local ignorance here, or situation-ally that it was Philadelphia area issue, but no, this is common all over the globe.

I was about to be sent from two days of partying about my freedom, to being completely ostracized within months. The gift that this second part became is so now lasting as agood for how

I would have never gotten out of that place without it.

Even the most hurtful things done to you by family can become a lasting good like this if you have the mindset to make it so.

The second night of partying at my parents house ended without any more outbursts and because Mikey was there now, I fought off the feelings of running away from it all from his being in my care.

I was going to do what I could to handle all of this I told myself. So there I found myself watching it all unfold, torn between real moments connecting again with love which I knew was still there in that house, and by the sad way it was born of. By evening time Mikey was done and had to be taken up to the bedroom.

I waited until guests left to go home to hang out with my brother upstairs as my parents got the house back together from the party down below.

Alone at last with Mikey upstairs in the back bedroom where Anna told me how things were with her the day before, my brother now looked a lot better for being cleaned up and shaved.

Mikey was in a lot of pain from his leg and unable to sleep he said, so I put a small portable FM radio on for us to listen to some music as we sat together.

We talked about how he waited for me to come home all week, and then he said that he was only going over to the local bar to get beer because he was so worked up from waiting for me that it was the reason he got run over in the road. I did not need him to defend himself for being a drunk, I just loved him and was glad that we now saw one another again.

As I sat beside his bed on a chair, I couldn't believe that I was there really. All the many days that I dreamed of my seeing my home again were never like this brutal truth.

I was flashing back to all of the things in this room he and I once spoke about as boys, it was breaking my heart that his life was so fucked up now. I just kept cherishing my brother being alive with me is best I could come up with.

My brother Mikey, legally known as Michael Silas Yarris, was born on December 31st 1959. Literally he was my idol growing up.

I know that's trite on some levels as to how so many bothers say such a thing, but not me. Mikey was the one who gave me my first pair of Converse Chuck Taylors basketball sneakers so that I would stop being bullied for wearing cheap knock offs at school. Mikey always stood up for me when kids bigger than I was picked on me. Mikey taught me to hunt and fish.

Quite literally Mikey was a champion of mine for all the days that I needed him to be there for me.

Now I was the "Big Brother' in stature between us, an unsaid thing that we both knew right then that I was to now be the stronger one of us.

Once more another lesson and, once more I knew what I had to try and become from each lesson as they came to me.

Sitting there, I didn't let on a single word about my diagnosis about my liver to Mikey. I did not have it within me to bring into this the whole overwhelming nature of things of just how screwed that we both were that night.

I eventually ended up in the basement alone on my what was my second night home. My ears were ringing from all the noise of the world outside, and as well I was wrung through from the many humans that were all around me that day.

My brain was screaming for rest, my eyes finally gave out, and I slept while I was curled up on the sofa in the basement with a blanket around me.

The thoughts about laying on the very spot where my brother Martin "MArty" Yarris had died never even got to me. I slept in the same cells in which men had committed suicide inside of them on the same day, so I was too hardened from Death Row to be mentally hurt by any situational settings.

In some ways I am bullet proof for what Death Row has taught me about myself. In only a few ways has if left

me scarred. I cannot cut my finger nails without a whole lot of courage from what was done to me with sheers by twisted guards who cut my nails for me. I will forever have an ability to drift off mentally to a place where I am gone, and the real world does not get through to me as well. That is how you shut out bad realities.

It is a shut down mechanism which I have with this second one that has protected me mentally from seeing things that sicken most.

I can't get rid of the memories of some of the killings that I witnessed in prison, nor stop picturing mentally some images of what the authorities did to men after a riot to fully go away. Some shit you can't not just unsee in your head when you have reminders in life bring them up.

My mother told me on the morning of the third day of freedom that she was taking me to a famous ice cream restaurant named "Bettys" for a treat for us non drinkers. She and I were the only ones who did not touch any booze.

Just her and I she said, and yet this all felt contrived somehow, ...not that she did not want me feeling like a

little boy who was getting a treat with his mother, this felt like it was time for her and I to talk about something she had on her mind.

I got myself together and went with my mother while wearing ill fitting shoes, clothes that were bought for me to walk out of jail wearing, and so much trauma of my getting out of jail that I was fragile mentally, but I needed to see this thing though with her.

Not once did I give in to wanting a drink, I did not even

take pain pills, so whatever I went through this whole way was straight of mind, and without an escape of any form.

My mother was a notorious "lead foot"...meaning her foot was heavy on the accelerator pedal.

Her style of stopping was full on, with your hands on the dashboard in front of you while bracing yourself for death. I was not happy someone trusted my mother with a V8 engine in a sports car with her being at age 73. Jayne was lit behind the wheel is what I am saying.

We got on the main road of interstate I-95 with my nerves shot from her many manouvers and I only relaxed a bit on the straight roads before us, as my mother was doing some mental matriculation's of thoughts, not paying me any attention as I pumped imaginary brake pedals...

As I watched and waited, she said out of nowhere; "Nicky I wanna show you something".

Since I did not answer her, she just went on with whatever she had up her sleeve. All now at way too fast speeds once she made up her mine to go hard at this decision she just made.

My mother then drove me to the shopping Mall located in the state of Delaware, to the very place where Mrs. Craig (The woman I was convicted of killing) was

abducted. Whoa, I was not expecting this.

As we pulled in to the parking area, my mother

began telling me about how she traced the route that the

killer took once he grabbed the victim here, and said how he drug her into her own car, after knocking her out of her shoes right where we had just parked.

I was not sure how to deal with this. Wow. Just nothing can prepare you for this immediate smack in the face that this is where someone was attacked that you paid for.

My mother took out a folded up white sheet of paper and

started to show me her diagram that she drew of things that she saw. And it was here was where the shoes were located she said. Then she pointed to how the killer then drove back into Pennsylvania to where they found the victim as she took me out of the parking area and towards Pennsylvania again.

My heart was in my throat thinking about my mother out on the streets being driven mad by a lie about her son like this. She was home feeding me dinner at the time of the crime, what else could she do when faced with such an utter truth.

There was no way my mother was going to believing any bullshit that her son had raped and then killed a woman and then had calmly sat before her eating a meal.

I was riding in the car with so much heartache for her pain, so much not wishing to be part of this moment. I mean it, I had just gotten a break mentally from carrying this lie for 23 years, this was too much too soon.

Still, with my wishing all of this would not be so, we next drove to the church where two boys had found Mrs. Craig in the snow the next morning after she had been murdered there.

I cried and kept my face turned away in sorrow for what I was feeling for that poor woman as my mother spoke about things.

I paid for that shit, I paid and I paid as each day they hurt me in prison for this crime. I tried to find dignity as they tried to break my heart for it all. I hated what I was having to feel while not hurting my mother right then for it.

I knew that on some deep level she had to do this display of how much she had fought for Mrs. Craig, how much she sought to help a fellow mother. Man, this was one of the most beautiful, yet truly shit moments that I have had to live through in gracefulness.

What a woman that she was, how fierce her love was for me, and lastly how huge her self worth to take on the entire justice system with little more than a truth which she knew to be her only shield.

They used to strip search my mother even though she was visiting me behind security glass to try and break her.

They would also make her wait all day, and let her have 15 minutes with me at times...they treated her like she was in on the murder, and that is one of the hardest things that I had to forgive them for doing.

I let my mother show me the place where they finally found the victims car after we left the church. Eerie how all three places were in a triangle, and all of this showing that whomever did this crime, intimately knew this one

five mile area very well.

This was the greatest display of a mother's love for her child that any man could be offered in life. What a woman.

In the end my mother said: "Look how they knew to get back into Pennsylvania on side roads, look how they knew this church parking area was so remote, look how they left the car afterwards with the doors locked, and with the lights inside left on for the police to find it that way"!

My mother said that as soon as she found the killers gloves were the one thing which the police hid from everyone else, that this was the biggest reason what made her never give up on believing those gloves held the truth.

I sat in utter awe of this woman as she showed me

physically what made her so determined to win. Got a shiver up my spine thinking how I nearly gave it all up once, and how I had nearly stolen all of her hopes with my desperate actions in prison.

This is why she came to me at one point and asked me to

stop fighting other men while inside, telling me that if I killed another man in there, I was taking away all of her dreams that one day she would come for me to take me home.

I was riding around in that car feeling shameful for how many times that I almost let my anger blind me to her needs outside. I rode beside then her wishing some how, some way, to show her it was all not a waste of her years of trying for me as well.

Honestly though, within only two days of being set free I had to learn how to become super strong mentally to deal with so many cruel layers of emotionally draining events yet to come.

The place that we were originally going to have ice cream treats at was closed when we eventually went there. We ended up sitting in a national chain restaurant and my mother spent the time there telling me about who I had met over the past two days at her house. She gave me all of the back stories to what, and also where they were now in life.

I let her go on talking, my hand not far from touching her arm and shoulder as she sat beside me while having her food. I had to tell her about my medical situation then, but I had to make it as upbeat as possible so iit was just news. I knew that was not fair to her to be hit with now, but we got through all the rest to that point.

So I told my mother that my renal output of my liver had gone critical in prison, and that my liver and kidneys were severely damaged. I told her as well that I had to not take pills or drink from being ill or I would die soon. I said that the doctors were very firm, and that they said I have a projected need for a new liver within a three years or so window from this point.

The look Jayne Yarris gave to me in response to this news was the one that humans make when faced with something so rejection-able that they screw their faces up in complete rejection of this distasteful thought.

I had big eyes waiting for what she was going to
say in response, yet still I got hit with her classic "Jayne Yarris summation" of it all.

It went this way:

"Oh Nicky, doctors know medicine, and doctors know books, but they do not know MY son!"

"You come home with me, I will make you my rich chicken soup that has the thick hand made noodles which I make. Then I will make your favorite breads as well".

"You eat my soup and the breads that I bake, and then you go walk until you can not walk any more. When you have gone as far as you can, then you come back to me and rest... I'll fix you Nicky, don't you listen to what anyone else says but me, do you hear me?"

Nodding in response as I feasted on her pride-filled words about who I was in her eyes, I determined then and there that I was damn sure not drinking. Neither would I take any pain pills, nor do anything but start to exercise and eat her food like she said.

My God, when I think about how, within my first three days of freedom, that I was mandated with duties and set up against challenges with life altering perspectives, I still have no clue why I was chosen for such a beautiful life after prison like this.

Yes, I mean it. What an amazing and beautiful nuance filled world that I found myself within right then.

It was so much like the ones where all of my days were spent dreaming about life in prison, about being so well connected again to my death row living, with each moment always this precious delight. It becomes so very addictive to live this way once you know it.

I was actually being handed in real time, tools to make me heal.

All I had to do was cling to a mannerism of which I could develop and use, all so that I could become the man out here I dreamed of being. Oh as well, by achieving this I would well have as a reward the ever present love of a woman who believed in me all along.

This was like some beauty of life which I had only read about in books, I had no idea before that moment that I was about to live one of the greatest "fable quality level of living" that anyone could imagine as being their own.

I was well aware that as the first man to seek DNA in America from Death Row, how this was remarkable on many levels, or that people would be enamored with the huge portions of my story about that one aspect if being on Death Row for so long.

Yet I would know all along personally, what a beautiful precious way that I would have to live my life, either with talking about being alive constantly, or infinitely seeking nuances to my life through levels that very few know even exists.

When others meet me, they are at times in wonder at the depth of efforts which I make to have a very unique perspective and outlook on things in life that I share with them.

Now you know that it is a driven effort from having to cherish each day as if it was truly my last one. In such a situation, the mundane is not on the your mind, you seek and hold onto the preciousness of all the tiny things each day can offer. Add to this what my mother gave to me upon release and you can see why I am shaped mentally in my life as I am today.

Thank God I was forced to live such a pious manner for years while in while in prison.

I was about to have a personal experience of rebuilding my life while trying to find my identity on top of this , all at the age of 42. That is the craziest thing that I ever thought I could write in life.

Litterally I had to find out who I was as a man out in the real world. I had to try and deal with having no money, no job skills, no work history or qualifications.

And as I was about to learn further the next day, no politician would help, not one government offer of assistance, and basically everyone still thought maybe I was the guy who scared everyone by escaping from Death Row while also having the sentencing judges' address in my possessions when I did.

I was soon after going to find out that I was to be preyed on by as many as could find me useful. All along I had to will myself to believe my mother, in that being polite and kind, eating her food while I exercised too, was all going to make it better somehow.

Now back to the rest I had to handle, with press and lawyers, or organisations who need someone like me to be set free so they can step out there.

Monday morning I went down to South Philadelphia and got a suit from a place named "Big Tony's Suit Shop". This was courtesy of a family friend who got me a huge discount on a floral patterned, light tan suit that made

me look like I was in camouflage that had faded in the sunlight.

This outfit was then topped off with, (and I cannot make this shit up)…a light brown Fedora hat that I used to cover up my hair loss. It all made me look like I was way out of step with this world of 2004.

With sallow skin, prison eyewear, along with that very diminished body from malnutrition, I was a then a weird

image of myself. I had no idea what I was, who I was, and what I had to say was not at all who I felt like inside. If you my reader can understand that complex offering of what I was dealing with, kudos to you my friend.

In a short while though, my being there was just that, I was back in South West Philly, I was back in the hood, and all around me I was the stranger to whomever I met there where I grew up.

I got up, ate whatever I could force down, I walked daily as I tried to not think about anything else but what I was seeing in front of me.

My first long walk lasted 4 blocks. My first jog took me a month, only for that to last me all of about 3 minutes of running flat out.

I was always in pain, I was always tired all day long, and I was experiencing moments not fair on me mentally.

I walked down to the woods near my parents house where I was raped as a boy one day without even really thinking of it.

I knew that the man who did it had family in the area and how a lesser man would think about getting back at him through them. I couldn't find the hate inside to be that way though. Just so sad how I had to have this done to me as a boy I felt.

I walked at night a lot when I got stronger, as I hated being indoors all day. I hated how I looked outwardly, so I got myself a black hoodie that was oversize for me to hide inside of. I would walk around at night hidden from all that way as I tried to heal.

The weather changed and got warmer, I was able to walk for a couple miles a day soon and doing light forms of exercise really helped. I even had my first sexual experience with a local woman who was one of my "corner girls" back from when I was a teenager that I was still close to.

I am not sharing that episode about my first adult encounter after I thought a lot about it, that was way too personal for me to share here in detail with this person. But mentally, it was just weird taking my clothes off at age 42 in front a woman who was then aged 45 (and a grandmother), and I was all kinds of not all right with this mentally because our bodies did not go with my brain. Does that make sense?

She could have been a gorgeous and wonderfully tall model who had a fit body, but it was too fucked up for me mentally, because I was the only one out of sequence in life as I tried to get an erection with this woman.

I was the only one walking around thinking that my last images of me at age 20 were still real somehow in or out of bed. That is the cost that I bore for not having a mirror in my cell, no ability to know what I looked like for so long that I simply had a shock of a moment when I saw some middle aged man walking around with my brain.

It was my walking around with a black hoodie on that got me a nickname of "The White Ghost" by the drug dealers.

Some local guys who operated at night nearby selling drugs called me this name. I didn't have any time for any bullshit and I don't flinch because you might be strapped up with a gun.

I was just in the joint with all of the leaders of any crew out here, and I had their respect and blessings. I was not afraid at all, just step back and let me be.

Seriously, anyone who knows America, knows that the streets are run from jail, and that the shot callers don't stop just because they are locked up.

I know guys who bought houses from inside jail for their family outside for how much money they made off of being in jail!

I would be out walking in the middle of the night when only the brave or desperate come out, I was determined to get in as much freedom as I could, while I hated being indoors. I couldn't go about this all scared is what I had to go though.

When I was not working on my plans for my "Economic Approach" to making Pennsylvania give up the Death Penalty, I was out walking. Some crazy things happen at night when you are out walking, and I got a tie between seeing a car engine being taken out of a flipped over car in a field by two guys, or a full on play gathering of children as young as ten or so in the streets just as if it were daytime, to be the best of what I saw on walks.

What was I up to with my economic speaking tour daydreams?

I had an idea about how to show these people that if you thought you squashed me like a bug, how I was going to show them that instead they had inspired me so much in life. Sitting in my parents basement only a few months free, I bet no one expected me to be on an international stage soon. That I would be there wowing others with a dictum driven oration skill set which they had never heard before. I knew I could do it.

Why did I believe that while sitting in my parents house, with no money, no resources other than a local library, that I could do anything in the face of what was done to me?

I sincerely was that guy inside prison whom others sought to help them to find a way through, or out of that hell hole which we shared. I was the man. I had stature and was looked up to by the ones who saw what I was capable of doing for others. If I could be than man on Death Row, then surely I could be than man here on the outside. That is all this was.

I reached out to a local University and within weeks I had a whole group effort going for me to go to the five biggest trade partners in the newly formed European Union, (which by charter mandates that trade is barred by any partner who executes its citizens), so I was off on this dream soon.

I know how I basically wanted to mess with their money by making a point and shame them as well, but I wanted to see just how bright I was now that I was out here.

I was joined on my EU trip in October of 2004 by fellow former Pennsylvania Death row Prisoner William Nieves, and Former Pennsylvania resident Ray Krone.

At the end of this trip, William would die from his own neglect due to Hepatitis-C infection which I shared with him as a condition, and Ray and I would never speak again from his hating on me.

This was one of those things that I set out with my ego to do some big time steps in life, only to see the folly of it all later. But man, what a ride it all was.

The plan was go to the five biggest trade partners and seek governmental help to force Pennsylvania to stop using this hideous form of punishment. I did hours of my homework learning about these things, and as well who to seek out on my trip for help from.

Great Britain had a company in the medical industry who had built a billion dollar building in downtown Philadelphia.

The same company was manufacturing the drugs that would be used to execute me. That was my crown jewel effort. This was long before anyone else came up with the idea of attacking the companys who made the drugs which were used to kill men in America on Death Row.

The Swedish Government was just then buying the old Philadelphia Naval yard for private ship building, they were on my list as well.

The Spanish Government, French, and Italian ones
were the next in line from there.

As long as William covered Spain with his language skills, we would all do well on this effort I thought at first. I wanted to try and use my many years of speaking in my cell to be a driving force on this trip.

What is this speaking I refer to here?

Looking at my situation at the age 21 as I sat convicted of murder and sentenced to be executed...this thought came to me:

I had one duty. I was going to die in the electric chair, but before they did that to me, they were required by law to let me speak.

The thought of that one aspect to my death made me so intimidated and afraid that I would embarrass myself, that I went on a driven mission to do one thing: The day that you all murder Nick Yarris, you will not see an embarrassing display of a broken human being.

No matter what, I was going to overcome the ugly and broken mannerism of speech which I was using at first. I was going to find eloquence and beauty in my words to offset their murder of me.

I swear to you, that is what made me stand before a lone
image of myself inside of my cell. It was a picture of me at age 17 holding up a fish I could with a huge smile.

Before that image I would recite the most beautiful written works ever created. The one need that I had for a mental accomplishment that was meant for my last dying moment, is my lasting gift to me now.

My beautiful voice was born of my desire that the sounds of my own last words were worth every effort.

So yes, I knew what my voice was gifted to do for me long before I stood before a combined session of the house of Parliament in England to "Speak" in October of 2004, just 9 months free from a Maximum Security prison cell.

I had such a beautiful command of speaking then that I knew something within me was extraordinary. All of it was simply way beyond what I ever saw of myself in life for sure. I fucking loved every bit of it.

I wholly admit now how I got off on this ability that I have to go on any platform and emanate a magnificence that is genuine. I am what I believe that I am so sincerely, that I have a deeply powerful impact on others because of it.

I took on all the infinite adaptions of behavior and mannerism of character to heart, so that so many others who wish to find this within themselves will somehow. That is what I offer them. I somehow become a beacon of that feeling to others who hear me speak for them to see a better version of themselves for it. I get that. I am well aware of the "Nick Yarris Effect" that I have on others.

By now 20 years on, this ability that I have in this one regard has become even more pronounced, deeper still for what I am as a man when I meet others.

It was so eerie to be on a European trip with William
Nieves, when the last time before I reunited with him there, was inside of Pittsburgh Penitentiary where we both sat under a sentence of death.

William and I each were infected with Hepatitis-C from the

same dentist back in Huntingdon Prison where we were both also housed, and we each had watched others die of this very hideous illness before he got out of jail.

When I followed William out of prison 4 years after his release., I saw that the huge difference between us was that William still drank booze, smoked, did pills, all while he did cocaine. I was all over him about that dumb shit when I first saw him in England, but he was all wrapped up in his own post release stress, so he could not hear me. I begged him to remember our days of being on Death Row, but he drank to forget them.

I hated how he died of not remembering what it was like to hold onto everything so preciously each day. I swore when he died right after this trip, how he gave me another reason to not squander my gift of being alive. I mean this, if you fight your heart out to get out of jail, and when you do get your life back, you don't just piss it away on booze and dope.

What bothered me was I even was forced to fight William in a cage in back in 1994, I knew him lik we were brothers who grow up together, this was not some total stranger to me whom I met then Ray was to met. Hell, I literally spilled had blood with this man.

It was during this trip in Europe that I started to next experience a phenomenon in my life that was unfolding before me.

Now this is where we are going to get into this thing that I will now describe and you accept what I offer as genuine, or you will think I am just making shit up.

Either way, here it is...

I went deep into a dark world while ingesting literally a poison in the form of pills called "Riboviron" that were fed to me by the medical staff in prison, while I was also being injected with a second poison called "Interferon" in by needle in an effort to kill the Hepatitis-C infection inside my body.

When I say I went deep, I mean not only did I feel horrible with bouts of clinical depression so severe that I wanted to beat my own face in for the misery which I then felt, but I also went into these dreams that were so unlike anything else that I had ever felt before.

I had riveting dreams of me at an advanced age, not the image of anything that I knew of my likeness I knew, and it was all so detailed and real. I will only remember these dreams again as each event that happened since release happened that were somehow tied to these dreams.

In my first days of being free I was met by the film makers of the Documentary titled "After Innocence". When I sat out back of my parents home and spoke to this film making crew, I tried then to speak about this all, but it never came out right. Basically, it can be like remembering an event but you were never there, seeing a car crash just a few minutes before one does crash. You only get seconds to recall when then has or did happen later. I always called it "Glimpses"... like I get a glimpse of my dreams while remembering also where I was when I had the dream, so all very double layered. Pretty amazing for how many times it has come about with witnesses to this happening in my life. It's what makes me able to tell it all.

Anyway, no. All of my my first efforts by me to talk about this phenomenon of my dreams was all lost to me being shown with a bullhorn, of me going to the courthouse where I was convicted within to go and protest on behalf of the victim. The authorities were not seeking the culprit of the crime with the same DNA that set me free being used to catch him, and I wanted everyone to knw this lame crap.

While I was in Europe, I kept being hit by some of the dreams that I once had on Death Row. The ones hitting me most was of me in a suit and tie, but I was outside in front of crowd at night, not indoors... because I saw the night sky above it all filled with the moon and stars.

Then all of that got shook off by the reality that I might have to go back to prison. Yes, just like that, head in the clouds thinking about dreams I once had and reality says hold on, you are not free.

While I was in France where I speaking before the French Government I nearly had to ask for "Sanctuary" under French law when my lawyers emailed me to then inform me that the state Appeals Court back in Florida had reinstated my 35 year sentence, and at that point,without an agreement with the Attorney General of the state of Florida, I had to go back to jail for 35 years.

Here I was thinking that I had my life back, and as hard as it was to live outside again, at least I have a few years of life with a damaged liver and two damaged kidneys I was telling myself.

Now I was thinking that I was going back to the worst setting of all and I was to rot away the last of my life in a jail cell.

My lawyer Peter Goldberger, worked out a deal quickly where the state of Florida is holding open my conviction right now to this day, (and should I ever come back and get arrested for any crime whatsoever), I have to serve out my 35 years that they say that I still owe them for my escaping to their jurisdiction in 1985.

To this day I am a convicted felon, and according to the state of Florida, they don't care that I served 23 years for a crime that I did not do, I will always owe them a whole new chunk of whatever is left of my life.

Call me insane for doing so, but I went to Florida three times since release. I just kept very much aware of my legal status there and then I got my ass gone as soon as I could each time that I visited.

In my first months of freedom I had no idea how my health would take a huge turn for the good on top of all of things. I was regularly going to a free sex clinic back in Philadelphia to monitor my blood infection. It was my fourth blood test of that year that revealed how I had a complete remission from my infection without any kind of additional medical treatments.

I literally went from near renal failure of my liver back in 2002-03, to a system so clean that I could donate blood right then, as I had near undetectable amounts of Hepatitis-C infection in my system.

I promise you that the unfolding of all this upheaval, against getting a clean bill of health was not lost on me. I was vacillating back and forth between so many feelings over it.

I really was changing, yet I so wanted this polyandrous sweet nature way that I had felt about life to be held onto for as long as possible. I was still shocked when I found myself alone at night while outside, looking up at what I saw of the stars. I still craved every mouth watering new treat that I came upon, and I so wanted to be in love. That was going to be hard and something far off for me I felt.

I was dating five different women at that time, and three were with someone else, so my personal life was a mess overly so, love was going to have to wait.

I am not making this up, this is what happens when you are a mixture of a Kipling character stuck in the complex setting of being also featured on the front of news papers everywhere when my lawyers filed a 21 million dollar lawsuit on behalf.

Once I had the headline "THE 21 MILLION DOLLAR MAN" plastered everywhere in the area, women soon found how out to reach me through my lawyers who had filed the law suit.

When everyone was sure that with a DNA based
exoneration from Death Rpw, (and how wealthy I was soon to be), I was uniquely the flavor of both young and middle aged women alike.

With sunlight and food, suddenly I had skin that was so youthful that I shocked others to say that I was 43 years old. I was so mature mentally that older women were enamored with my charm and elegant manly manners.

Oh I admit it, I was making up for not being touched by a human hand for 15 years big time! I was making up for all of the longings and lonesome feelings that I had to endure with unabated zeal.

I told each one about the others I was dating, I was making sure that I played fairly. Made a point to tell all about how I had just gotten my life back, and that I was just sharing time with them each. I just wanted to have some fun before I left to wherever it is that I would find my home to be in life. All my efforts were not enough to stop jealousy and petty acts though. I paid for this dearly in time...

Being a very love-able man can be so addictive to some one who's not had a man be so attentive to them. It is so good that they just have to wreck that shit when it is no longer theirs to have.

I have had that act done to me so well my first year out of jail that I stopped ever trying to date like that again.

The whole real reason I had to finish this aside on this point was because of an incident that changed my heart about all of this dating crap that happened while I was in Europe.

So there I am in Italy at one point, my dreams start hitting me like real memories from shit long before then, against why I have to worry about being sent back to jail.

Couple all that with how all the while I had to watch William drinking his life away, it was draining. I kept having some eerie feeling that I would be back in Rome again, but on my own next time.

It began to get deeper still when I met a man whom I was sure that I knew in my dreams years before.

Carlos was his name, he was part of a religious group that all the others on tour with me did not want to hang out with. It was boring for the others travelling with me to go to church and pray with our hosts, they did not want to spend time with them all hardly. They all went off to go sightseeing, while I went and prayed and then absorbed the offerings of being grateful for life.

I was staying in the villa of the author Thomas Cahill, who wrote the satire titled "How the Irish Saved Civilization", which eerily enough, I had actually read while I sat on Death Row.

The villa in Rome has a kitchen which had a window that was facing another flat's kitchen window across a devide of about twenty feet wide.

After I met Carlos in church, he came over to where I was staying and gave me a coffee maker.

It was one of those expresso ones you put over a fire. I told him how I could not wait to make coffee the next morning in this thing. Little did I know that wisp of a dream about a man in a beard who handed me a silver object, was all now part of my dreams I had under deep medication, when I was near to death. I just knew this man somehow.

And just like a very distinct dream I once had, It was here in this Villa in Rome that I had the most romantic and beauty driven events of my life come about for me.

Me and my coffee. Its one of my few besides ice cream. Ah, the delicious coffee bean. I had to learn how use this funky Italian espresso coffee maker on the stove that first try, got it done as best that I could. I also found honey in the cupboard, and had milk to go with it from the fridge. I was set and was so grateful for my first coffee in a while.

I stood sipping my very strong cup of coffee that I used way too much grounds to make one cup, so it was do-able but not great. Just then I saw a woman in the kitchen across from me making her own coffee.

I smiled seeing the flames under her coffee maker, thinking how she probably did not use 6 big spoons of coffee grounds to make hers like I stupidly did...

I stood and just watched until she had her cup made, thinking it was so like a memory of how she held her cup, yet I never saw this person before then in my life.

When she turned and faced me across this small open area between us that had laundry hanging on lines that

were crisscross the outside of our windows, she smiled brightly at me.

We were up on the second floor of the villa, above the street that was full of sounds of traffic below.

I couldn't speak to her, I did not know if she spoke English, I knew only food words in Italian, so this was all going to be a silent moment which we shared looking at one another as we drank coffee together.

I remember so finely how, when we finished our drinks,

how she set her cup down on the left of her window sill as she smiled at me in this unique way.

I took the cue and set my cup down on the right of my window, as if they then were together.

With our cup handles in opposite direction, I bowed

slightly and left, as she in turn dipped her head... she did that one where one side of a girls' head tilts down, that eye on that side of her face smiles sly-like at you? You know the one as only a girl can do?

That is what she did to perfection right then.

All day long, I replayed the morning with her in my head as I walked around Rome. Detail after detail of her were just there in my head for some reason. I could not help but feel like somehow I had seen her before.

I kept seeing her eyes, the lovely rich chestnut

colored hair.

I saw again in my head her lovely slender neck, the way her shoulders fitted with her torso, to the lovely way she used her arms…I just floated around Rome thinking that was some cool ass romantic stuff to do with a woman.

The next morning I was back just about that same time in the kitchen as the day before, and yes she did show up.

Oh, yes that hair is not left to a single stray, make-up is flawless in that you barely know she has that eye shadow on until she looks down. That is when those eye lashes flutter just briefly like they are meant to.

This woman was prominently statuesque, and if this was some crazy dream of mine for just getting out of jail, or if she was in my dreams while on Death Row, then yes either way more of this please!

Same thing again on day two of my coffee driven new romance, with the smiles, the looks and the way we set our finished cups down in exactly the same way all followed on our second encounter

I knew by day three with this woman of this lovely and sweet exchange, when she and I ventured into "flirtatious eye contacts", accompanied by lascivious smiles of knowing… all made this like the coolest ever non contact event with a woman that any man could find himself having.

I was hooked, and I wanted so badly for her to crook her finger and invite me over to her, but yet at the same time, I just wanted this to have one last time to be perfect for us.

I did this thing mentally right then, where I started picturing how I could hold onto something that was really beautiful.

All I had to do was not push it, not try to go fuck this woman and by doing so fuck this all up in the process. No I wanted to make this all a lasting good.

On my last morning there it only changed at the end when I waved goodbye. My coffee companion looked pained for understanding that this was the last time. I stood right at the glass and I kissed the glass gently.

In turn she smiled at me and touched her lips as if my kiss had flown through the window somehow to reach her. I tipped my head, smiled one last time, and then I left.

I never saw what she did as I did not turn back. I never stopped feeling like that was the way she wanted me to act, like I did the best version of this

interaction. We each got to keep something so simplistic and complexly beautiful just between us, only there in that kitchen.

From that day onward I truly always wanted to feel this way about someone in real life. I just knew that if I could

have this type of connection with someone who loved me,then all my efforts to find life's joys would be so magnified that I would be breathless to talk to them for having such a bond. I mean this one thing more than anything else in life.

The title of this book is derived form the offering to mind one's heart, because it is truly only with our mind that we then break our own hearts for the thoughts which we created over love.

This is what I mean about what was happening to me in Italy. The people the others on tour had no time for? They loved me so much they asked me to do them a huge favor. They asked me could be this beautiful man who is happy to be free from Death Row before a huge crowd? Could I do this on stage at the Coliseum with 20.000 human beings assembled there for meto speak to them?

My jaw hit the floor when I was asked to come back to Italy on my own in November of 2004 to do a once in a lifetime event of Speaking at this iconic location which the whole world knows.

The rest of my tour was draining at times because Ray was envious of my speaking. I swear, I am over it all now, but dude just hated on me.

The rest of the group ditched me on the last morning in Holland. Oh yeah it was that lame of a try, only for me to beat them to the airport in a taxi and stare them down in line for our tickets to the UK to all be approved.

Then when we land in the UK, I get bumped up to first class on our flight (all because my neighbor was a flight attendant on my flight with them from England to Philadelphia), so I was not even wasting any words on them as we came back.

I had a really deep moment come about because of all of this international speaking. I learned that I was always better off not speaking in a group if it meant the amount of years one spent had some validity to be envious about. I did 23 years in solitary confinement on Death Row. Ray served 2. When I spoke about my strife he felt that I overshadowed his own story. That is all this was.

I had no preparations for something so huge an ordeal for my second trip to Rome in 2004, but I knew what to do, it was in their question to me.

The whole celebration that I was asked to take part in was about Italy giving up the Death Penalty, some 150 years before that date in November when I'd be there.

It was about Italy, It was about a people wanting to never face things like this the way America is dealing with the Death Penalty.

All I was needed for was simple I thought: Be the image of a newly set free Death Row prisoner who is grateful to be alive.

Here again, all sorts of times in Italy, my dreams from long before kept haunting me making me feel I was so sure that I had been there as another soul. Madness to want to believe any of it, but I was living this event with this sensation that was so real.

When the event came, I hope this next part gives credence to what I mean.

I worked with an interpreter to do my presentation in
Rome. I had down what I was going to do. But the lead up to what I said was awesome.

After the Mayor of Rome told the audience his pride in
human rights, and how they rid the country of the scourge of the Death Penalty, an Italian Actor with a rich baritone voice read the poem titled "The Executioner" by Leo Tolstoy to perfection in English. He eloquently was hitting all the layers of this written work beautifully.

Then the assembled gathering was told that they were
about to meet a man who had just gotten his life back from the gallows thanks to DNA evidence, and that his message for all was love…

Wearing a lovely black suit of clothes that looked painted on my frame, I approached the stage while a dozen children who were kneeling down in a line behind me then released white Doves from boxes they all held before them.

I walked with dignity to the Microphone where my interpreter stood. I waited the longest
few moments as the applause died and they waited. I drug that next bit of silence out as long as I could bear this minute.

Then I began: "To My Italian family before me tonight and all others here, thank you@.

"I want you to know that if this is all but a dream, and I wake up back in my cell tomorrow, It does not
matter to me, as I am going to live this one night as if it my only night to be alive",

Thank you and good bye"…

It was then that I waited another long moment with my

head down, and I then turned and walked off of the stage to an applause that cried out for my leaving, wanting that not to be it so.

That was one of the best things they could have touched…the joy of a man who knows only to be gratefully free and joyously alive.

When I left the stage I was shot through with energy. I was caught between feeling totally vulnerable, to this sense of massive accomplishment. I hid from everyone, as I left through a side gate meant for the performers.

I ended up in the quiet streets of Rome with all the fanfare of the event still thumping off in the distance behind me as I walked.

I did not want to stay and have a perfect moment made mundane by hanging out and conversing all night. I wanted to just not do anything to ruin one of the best days a man like me could know.

To be an image of beauty and eloquence, to have so many people look at me as they did was mine to hold onto as I walked all night through Rome. No one I saw even noticing me, as I needed it so.

When you are thrust into something this big just a few months out of prison, this is a test for you to not get your mind blown on so many levels. I went from all this romance driven silence with a woman whom I never saw again, to this staged event where I was fucking Batman! I was this mysteriously elegant figure that left like a wisp of smoke as they were all left in wonder as to who I could be.

That is a whole lot for some street kid from Philly, who read a ton of books and taught himself to speak aloud for the pitiful sake of not dying in ignorance to pull off I thought.

I might have had the most glorious moment on the stage at the Coliseum, but it took a whole lot of mental acuity to handle it without being mentally off from it all.

61

Want to know what really got to me? The silence in the aftermath.

I did two months touring Europe, followed by one of the grandest events that a man could be central to in Italy, to then go back to the ghetto. I had to go be in the hood, where it is all broken down, and it is drab to the point of painfulness.

I hated being so free to be internationally a totally different me, one full of offerings of life, only to then come back to a place where that's a foreign idea to all. It was crushing to feel all of this. I was living in a rented room of a friend who offered it to me when I got back. I couldn't live in my parent house. I gotta explain though, it's not their fault.

My parents had their home broken into so many times they had dead bolt locks front and back of the house. If I was out after they went to bed about 9, or 10 o'clock, I could not get in the house unless I woke them up or climbed the back patio porch and came in through the kitchen door.

Trying to sneak a date into my folks house under such conditions was stupid and embarrassing for a man my of age. I knew that I couldn't stay there. Thankfully my friend Vincent let me have a room to rent in his house that was just outside of Philadelphia.

I would sit in the rear bedroom of Vincent's house for days being so drawn to whatever happened in Italy. I just could not believe what I had experienced, and no one in my life around me was able to understand it.

Less than a full year of freedom and it felt like I was out here for much longer. "Just keep your promise to Jayne, and keep on going Nicky" I said many days there.

CHAPTER THREE: MONEY IS LIKE THE WEATHER.

My first Job when I got out of jail? A local wanna be mob guy who had a rented garage in my neighborhood asked me to come see him about a job. This guy that I once knew years ago, now did the car detailing for all the local criminals in the area. He told me to come see him if I needed money. When I showed up, I was told how I could work off the books cleaning the shuttle buses at the local airport.

I would get 10.00 dollars per bus that I cleaned. I was told that I usually would clean 6 to 7 buses per day. I took the job as I then gave my parents money for my staying there and feeding me. I was still weak and sick, but I had to try and help myself. I lasted two weeks working there because I walked into the garage one morning and a car in there had a trunk full of machine guns. That was the breaking point. Cops come and raid, I get done for being part of a criminal conspiracy, so no thank you.

So, I decided to try and do speaking for money after that job was a waste of effort. I got my first gig offered to me from a local group. I borrowing my mothers car to go drive early in the morning to go and speak at a Mennonite Businessmen s' meeting that was to pay me 35.00 dollars for my efforts. (Plus free breakfast of course). I did okay, but I really could'nt see me doing local speaking about crime or justice.

That is when I then sought the creation of the huge International speaking tour which I shared with you earlier in this book.

I came back to Philly after all that and now back here, just before Christmas my first year out, I was struggling.

No job, no funds, nothing but a few speaking gigs at schools since my trip to Rome, it was not going well for me. I was driving a 1989 Jeep Wrangler that was given to me, while I was living in the house of a friend I hardly even knew. So to be honest, I wasn't sure where my life was going.

That's when I met Karen. She came to American just
before Christmas and met me in Philadelphia. I so wanted my series of dating local women to end, as it was going badly with one woman who would do her utmost to submarine my life when I tried to leave Philadelphia.

Karen... I met only a couple of women during my EU trip. Only two of them asked me for my phone number. I was completely taken by surprise that a woman from England would ring my phone and tell me they met me in London and now were here in America.

I was still so enraptured by that whole international "Me" experience just a month before, that I thought this encounter was to be magical like Rome was, or somehow all part of my dreams.

One phone call led to many that first day, then Karen said she was changing her flight to stay an extra two days as she was driving to see me in Philadelphia. She got a hotel room at the airport and after I finished my last speaking gig of 2004 set up by Peter Goldberger at Haverford University, I drove straight over to see Karen.

Once done speaking I went to the hotel room Karen had rented and for hours I sat by the window in the room on a chair just talking to her.

I listened to Karen rationalize to me how my chances of survival here in "Killadelphia" where there are some 500 murders a year were bleak. That instead how she could offer me a better life in England if I left here. I let Karen convinced me that with her high flying job, that she could give me a chance to be someone better than this

place would allow me to become. She said that when she hear me speaking in London it was like nothing she had ever heard before.

I wanted so much for this to be as magically true like

Rome was, that I started to just believe this was all meant to be. I leaped at the chance to get out of there.

I got on an airplane two days after I met Karen, and I left America.

That's crazy right? You meet a woman who tells you all this wonderful painted image of what your life could be while you are broke, barely even able to believe in your ability to get out of this very horrible setting?

I am never going to degrade any of this encounter, nor will I say that I fucked up by doing this crazy thing where I literally walked out of my life for the promise of a person whom I had just met. It led to me having a beautiful daughter.

What happened between my leaving Philadelphia and her birth, on to her being estrangement to me now, are all some things that I am not wasting a whole lot of writing on. I refuse to feed an ego like Karen's by making this work about her dumb shit actions between us.

So just for fairness to this being a cohesive rendition of

the factors leading to now, here is how it went...

I was not aware that just because Karen said to me that her and her man Angelo were finished, and that they were just friends by then, that it did not mean what she painted this picture to be in reality.

Angelo was currently living in their house that he shared with her, and they also had a poodle dog named Coco together. This was no plug and play situation, I was having to hide out in hotel rooms near the house and then be hidden in Karen's parents house while she worked out how to even tell Angleo that it was over. Oh yeah, she did not tell him before I landed in England, and it was about a week into my being there that she actually went to the house and told him it was over.

Oh yes it did, it burned to go from one dysfunctional family setting to another as Karen and her folks had all sorts of issues as well. Not as drink driven and vulgar as my family, but just as screwed up. Within days of my being there I saw the other side of this thing being nothing like Rome. I was so getting disheartened about it all.

This all got really messed up from where it all began with me all romantic and happy on a flight to a new life in England, only to see that I ended up with no choice but to keep going with this all.

The following events are right out of a Sydney Sheldon novel for the many layers going on all at once. I was sadly the besieged lead character being driven by a narrative that is not his own making obviously.

I made the mistake of not realizing that my being kind in my parting ways with one woman whom I was dating back in Philly was not in reality, just ammunition for her to seriously get back at me for leaving.

While I was in England this woman who was first pretending to be such a caring friend who wished me happiness in my new life, listened to me by phone tell her what I was facing in my new life and how I was not so sure of things. This in her mind gave her an idea that if she ruined things for me in England, that I would come back to be with her or near her. So unfair, but really true that this ex girlfriend went to my parents house after talking to me. Right at a gathering in front of others in my family this woman told my parents she spoke to me that very day.

My ex from Philadelphia then said how she learned that I was living with a woman who had just finished living with a black man back in England.

I'm being nice here in my writing this, but you know the word which she used when she drove this dagger home with both fists into my back. The only reason she knew his skin color is because I had shared how Angelo's brother was a famous musician whom the world knew was a black man.

My parents were embarrassed and hurt by this shitty act, and all my mother would say later when I called home, was that they needed to talk to me because of what this woman was going around telling everyone. I could tell by her voice that my mother wanted no parts of this spiteful act.

Still, I dreamed of a Christmas at home for so long that I blanked all of this horrible reality and I went home my first year out of prison, even after this incident just a week earlier...

I got a flight on December 20th 2004 from England and by the time I landed in Philadelphia I had nothing left to come back to there, no matter what happened to me back in England with Karen.

When I got to my parents house and I was told to get the fuck out at the front door by my father, I blanched. I asked him why. I was told that I was not welcome to stay there, that he did not want me bringing all this trouble to his house. My trying to get out of Philly was trouble. Like really?

That was the closest night that I ever came to going to going off to get drunk in all my time out of jail. I really was so destroyed that this ex girlfriend had not only hurt me, but she had ruined my first Christmas out of jail, all while she made Karen hate my parents. She left me in a situation that ruined any chance that I had to be happy.

When I left my parents house I got on my mobile phone and I called this woman who did all of this and asked her

why. Why would you gleen all of this information from me, only to then turn around and use it like she did? She pretended that she didn't even know she had even said it, and made out like I was being a dick for even going to be with some "Jew Bitch" as she shouted at me as she hung up the phone on me.

See what I mean about how, even as I began my life in freedom, how all of these many factors kept it all from having any chance for me to be happy? Find healing? Really.

So how was I supposed to figure out who I amidst all of this chaos others were causing me? I was being torn apart by so many unfair things mentally about just living in freedom , so how cruel was all this?

It was not pretty, fair, nor even right what was being set up for me by everyone around me...all of whom at one time or another professed so much love for me! That's the part hardest of all to deal with later, and the following points are showing any here reading this why I did all the many things that I did from this point onwards.

I was so offended that I did not have the courage or brain power to defend myself. I stood like a mute listening to how it was better that this is my last trip there, and how I was to keep my mouth shut to my mother about all of this. She was going to go along with it, with her eyes shut to whatever was ugly and stealing her dreams, all just to keep the peace at home. I understood that. Women will just let things go for the sake of no more yelling and fighting.

It really sucked to be me right then. How I did not end up going off and getting smashed on booze, I still don't understand to this day. I never felt so humiliated as I did walking away from my childhood home knowing that any dreams I once had in prison were just that...dreams.

I gathered enough courage and I tried on Christmas eve, even though I was feeling wrecked emotionally, to go to their house and at least share presents that I had bought back in England for my mother and father.

I was so aware of how awkward it was in my parents house after I gave them their gift wrapped boxes, that I asked if could I just stay in the basement for a while and watch Television until it was late enough for me to go to sleep at a friends house who was letting me sleep on their sofa.

I told my parents that I could get my bed set up when their family went to sleep, so I hoped they did not mind if I stayed for a bit. I went down stairs and sat on the sofa where Marty died and I thought about my first year of freedom.

I was down there going through a catalog of the events from when I got first out of jail and I was sitting down there in this very spot, to what I was doing there now. While I sat there in silence I never even noticed that the house had gone completely empty upstairs.

I wanted to cry for how fucked up it was when I went upstairs and asked my niece (who's partner was in prison for bank robberies) where my parents were, only to learn that they went out to my sister Anna's house for the party they were all having.

I was not invited to go and they all decided to quietly leave me down in the basement while they left for a party. This wasn't her saying it like she went along with it, she just kindly told me how Anna called my parents while I was downstairs, and how Anna told them to come over and not to let on about their leavin as a big deal.

When I think now about how my entire family left me sitting in my parents basement on my first Christmas home, I am still so proud of myself for what this all was to come to mean to me personally.

Sitting down there in the very spot that my little brother died on a few minutes later, I didn't ball my eyes out with feeling sorry for myself.

I didn't feel anger or unjust things to make my ego feel rewarded. I sat there and gave this shit some serious thought. Okay, my own family thinks that I broke code, that I somehow went somewhere and was someone
they now cannot see.

How weird that I somehow am not like my family on so many levels that I have to be ostracized, that I have to be shown a cold shoulder.

I did the only sensible thing any clever man could do. I went upstairs and got out my mother's phone book and I got my sister Anna's address from within it.

I then rang Karen up on my phone and woke her up at like 2:am. I asked her to help guide me over the phone by reading the maps online that were leading to Anna's house from my parents house. I used this help for me to find my sister's house.

I swear to God, I had no ability to get there at night and find a street out in the county where Anna now lived, there was no Google maps like today. I just used the best idea that I could come up with...have a navigator direct me along the route via the phone.

When I got to my sister's house my parents were just then leaving. It was a cool set up that just as I was about to actually knock on the door, it opened right then. Right there was my parents saying good night.

That set it up so that those at the door saying a jovial farewell to my folks had to then turn and welcome me as if I wasn't the one they had all ditched to go have a drunken party.

I smiled and walked in to Anna's house knowing none of the men would cause a fuss, I am top dog like that in the family, and the women all present knew what they did to me was wrong, so everyone was overly kissing my ass.

I went down to the basement where the main party was being held and I told them all goodbye when I got them all to listen to me.

I said to everyone that Karen was still on the phone to me in an ear piece which I was using to stay on the call that we had used to guide me there.

I said that I was fine with what they wanted of me, and that I wished them all the best after that night. I did this very pious thing where I said not one negative thing as I got away from them all that night. I swear though, I spit on Anna's front door when I left.

I literally turned at the porch felling so sick inside for what was just done to me. I turned around and while looking at the house, I spit on their front door in anger at what had happened with my family.

How could any family ditch someone who had just came so close to dying in prison, travelling thousands of miles to to just see you all again?

I swore then and there that I was not living in any location they would be living. I was not going to forget this shit was done to me, as it was a huge gift to me.

I mean it. Had I not been rejected by my own family, I would have probably told Karen no thank you to living in England now that everything was all smeared.

I was not liking how I felt being in Angelo's house, sleeping in his bed, playing with his dog, or while I fucked his woman there. I felt like a shell fish that just took another creatures shell, and now I have to walk around feeling like shit because no matter what, it is stolen.

I did not share with my family how hard Karen being on me was back in the UK, and that twice from arguing with her, I had gotten booted out of her car in England.

I had to stand there for hours at the place where she chucked me out at, hoping that eventually she came back to get me. Literally learned my lesson in that I was only one stupid mouthy comment away from being shown the door.

I am not feeling sorry for myself, I know what I went through is as messed up of a "Welcome Home" as one can get smacked in the face with, but I also know as I write all of this now, that I did some rebellious shit in retaliation for being on the end of a dancing string from Karen.

I am not totally without blemish, I just feel sad that I let myself fall prey to a lower self that I was at times.

I told myself then the rationalizations which I held for why I did things were real and, I used all the validations I felt inside that I needed for why I did things wrongly. I just am as stupid as anyone else like that.

What I am saying is, I made shit worse with my own actions as to what was already a fucked up situation and boy did that cost me as well.

If you think what was done to me in Philadelphia by an ex girlfriend who decided to wreck my life for leaving her was bad, wait until you see what Karen next did to me all because I loved her and would leave her.

I have had enough time and self reflection at this point to share things about this next part that are both fair and honest.

They will be brief though, I swear to all above that I am not stroking her ego with a prolonged scribe about her in my life. In total I would be married to Karen for less than three years, and that's about the sum total of my interactions with her outside of court battles for my daughter Lara Rebecca Yarris.

Oh yeah, things are anywhere but on a good track for long in my life like this…

I get over being played the fool by my family and I go back to England only to get thrown back to America at

the end of February of 2005 to go to the "Sundance Film Festival". I got my family to come to New York City in January to witness Karen marry me in New York City so that I could get my immigration in England done. That's the only reason they agreed to come.

I literally stood in a hallway in New York next to a pregnant teen, as well as various immigrants who were in line for there chance to have a ten minute civill ceremony for whomever they were marrying. The cost 99.00 dollars for each couple and you got one free photograph taken by the city employee.

Parted ways with my parents and my brother Mikey in New York, and I go with Karen (who ditched work and would lose her job over this) to go to Utah to be part of "After Innocence" film competition at the Sundance film festival.

Getting back to a similar setting as Europe, I found myself trying to emulate that magic. I end up having a cut loose time from all this family drama by being this larger than life person who takes on the judicial system with a bull horn in this film. Everyone who watched the film "After Innocence" was so amazed to meet me there in the streets during the festival. I met the many film stars I watched in film or TV while they knew who I was. That blew my mind. Soon I was invited to sit at this huge table with Steve Buscemi and his son, I even ended up throwing snow balls at others in the parking area below the place that we were all in, along with the cast of the film "Good Fellas"!

I had dinner with Hollywood stars who blew me away with

some of their work. What a treat to be part of something so big. What a crazy thing to have thrown at me mentally only to go back to England later and be back in a little village called London-Colney.

That is when I go hit with the thought... "Now what the hell do I do after I been places like that"?

I was driving a motorcycle around because I was a bit over matched with the physical switch of the steering wheel on the right, and then having road system on the left.

I did the smarter thing and learned the road systems on a Motorcycle so that I had it down and passed my UK driving test on first try. But that motorcycle was not good for work in winter.

So, with total Philly flavor to my way of doing things, I built a cage on my motorcycle so that my buddy Coco could ride on the back.

I went to Hyde Park, over to Speakers Corner, and I would perform my speeches there as if I were front of the Governments who I spoken to before.

I did not do this for money, After what I saw of myself on film in Utah, I wanted to be the finest speaker in the world so that my message was heard. I had no agent, no one to help me do any of this, so I was going to practice as many days that I could here at the park, until I built myself up enough to carry this message further.

It was this mindset and this effort that led to the whole change that my life next took. It was one woman who heard me speaking who then told me how I had to speak to her husband back in Australia. She said that it was he who had a radio show that would be blown away to hear me. Glenn Gary is the man's name. Never forget his name for some reason, juust always easy for me to remember how this one man changed so much for me.

Anyway, yes I said, and I did a wonderful interview with Glenn expressing my joy in finding myself in England after such a life back in the USA. I pointedly told all of the good parts of this new life which I had here.

Little did I know that the BBC back London listened to that show, saw its audience response to me and then they contacted me about doing one of the biggest BBC4 radio programs of the day that was titled "The Choice" with Michael Burke.

I worked with a producer for months named Katherine Blannerhassett going over my story in detail, and she did so well with me during this time that when I was in the studio, Michael Burke sounded as if he knew my story so

well. This interview was like it was two close friends going over the fascinating parts of an over all huge story on a level above the average story sharing never holds for the listeners.

That recording went wild across the BBC platform. It was actually replayed three times in one day. I next got

hundreds and hundreds of messages sent to my first website, with all manner of offers which came through.

Karen did brutal battles with all the females who wrote me as she was running my website by then, like mostly all else in the house that she controlled.

It was not easy to explain but I let Karen run me. I wasn't who I am now during my first year home, I was not able to define myself enough to handle another person's machinations over you as well as I can today.

That had to come as I got stronger, and i was not freaked out by the prospect of being homeless. This was one of those first steps towards this freeing myself from bad situations.

Three distinct things came out of this event. Each one of them was like a dream being answered. It was sunny and bright as I thought about each one.

Firstly I got an offer to be an author by literary agents were wanting to help me to sell my first book.

Secondly, I got a job offer to be working for a human rights charity in central London.

And then finally, I got an offer to make the film Documentary which would be titled "The Fear Of 13".

I knew that I had talent enough to do a very unique story telling if someone gave me a fake Death Row cell, so that I could show everyone where I came from.

To be given a chance for a stand alone film to be like "After Innocence", and have it be featured back at Sundance was all amazing.

I knew that if millions of listeners were blown away by me simply doing 29 minutes about the choice which I made be executed rather than linger on in sorrow on Death Row, then I knew I could be better.

I just had to now find a message of development that worked for my first book while I worked on this new film project.

It would be easy to do the charity work that I got hired for as I was promoting another platform as a hired spokesperson, but what was my own message to be?

I had to shape my first book so that it focused solely on my own personal development as a man against the backdrop of being wrongly convicted and sentenced to die. If I could keep the book focused there, then anyone can appreciate someone poorly educated, who then tries to use their own efforts of development to face a brutal life situation.

When I started off writing my first book, I came to a decision. My story is so crazy that I had to actually keep a huge segment of my story truncated, so that I stuck to what really mattered to my first book... The simple act of showing what it took to derive an educational effort that made me master Death Row.

This was the precarious time for me then in England, the one that brought me so close to having everything come my way in splendor, only for this next "crash and burn" episode to go really wildly off the rails for me.

The only bright spot through this all was the birth of my daughter In April of 2006. I was full time caregiver to her for the first year of life, I took her all over the world on trips just the two of us while I wrote my first book.

I loved her assiduously, so Spain, France, America, I had money by now, real money. I wrote my first book with Lara and I in some of the most amazing places a child could go with her daddy. Karen was off spending the money she got from my settlement, and we get to that next, but this time with Lara was my redemptive good

that I sought. I poured myself into being her daddy in every good way, but then things went haywire.

Part of the reason I always had Lara with me was because Karen had developed post natal depression. And what with her having an aggressive personality to begin with, things got nasty. A set of car keys to my face in her kitchen was the final straw. I don't care what anyone says, being attacked while holding a child while being a man is the most gut wrenching thing.

I decided that was enough, I couldn't allow a child to be exposed to verbal outbursts brought about by fits of contrived jealousy to scar the baby.

It was for this very reason that I ended up settling my lawsuit with Pennsylvania for a quarter of what I should have been paid. I lost nearly half of the settlement amount of 4 milion dollars to my lawyers who got the law suit filed, anther chunk went to a conversion rate of 1.9 to the British Pound for US dollars in 2008 when the markets crashed. Oh, and then after all of that loss, I gave Karen 1 million dollars for Lara Rebecca to be raised. Karen said the UK courts would give her half, so I then negotiated my freedom for 1 million dollars so that no matter what, Lara would be okay. That left me with about 700 thousand pounds for what I endured over 23 years of Death Row.

But despite such a huge payment and loss to be free of the dysfunctional madness with Karen, I got the fuck out of her house. I got a one bedroom cottage to rent In Stevenage England that overlooked a field with horses. I got the biggest set of speakers on a stereo system and I went to work on my film project, book and Human Rights charity speaking. I had a book deal despite Karen nearly blowing it by having someone ghost write my book for me, and I was determined to write 7 Days To Live my way.

Karen took the money from my settlement that she got from me and went to go buy property in Dubai with her girlfriend, I then started taking Lara rebecca all over the world in my new BMW car, or on flights across the globe.

Want to know how long "Living the good life" lasted for me? I moved into that little cottage in January 2008. I would be living in Holland 9 months later.

That one choice that I made to leave Karen and try to be happy by trying to be with someone else?

Oh no, that was not allowed to be real to someone who would show a pathological effort to show me why no one ever leaves her in life.

This was the onset to a series of paybacks that are still as I write this new book today, are ongoing from Karen even now.

I swear to all who are reading this work now that
Karen might be a lot of things, but a quitter on revenge she is not.

In short order this is how it went:

Found out I was dating a young woman. Karen came to my house when my idiot house guest told me upon my returning from the local shops with milk and bread, how my wife had called. When she got to the part where she that Karen was " so nice to her" I knew what was coming.

Before I could yell at this woman for answering the phone, before I could tell her to get her coat, and lets get out there, Karen was at my house. She jumped out of her car with Lara in the baby seat up front next to her, came to the door and began trying to kick in the door.

That was who I was dealing with. Cool for her to date, but nah, not anyone allowed to be with me. I really had to deal with all of this while writing my book, do my job, or work with the film crew.

Despite a really empty personal life, I tried to just keep believing thaat if I wrote the book, got the film done, I could just launch my career and have enough money for life.

When I did complete the book and the publishers thought I was gifted enough to give me 100 thousand UK pounds for my manuscript I celebrated. I did it all on my own without a ghost writer.

Flying high on my own efforts I went with my daughter Lara in July of 2008, to go to Florida with her to stay at Disneyworld resort, with me flying my parents in from Philadelphia first class so that we all could have a week long celebration of my first book being

released.

Karen celebrated this when she broke into my home back in England while I was in Florida.

Karen got ahold of that woman whom she tried to break into my home and beat down, got her to tell Karen how to creep into my house via the back fence, so then Karen climbed the rear fence and broke into the cottage and she found some pot plants growing in my garage.

Yes, rather than commit a crime on the streets I tried to grow a small amount in my garage.

This then got me arrested at gunpoint when I got off the flight. Karen was at the airport with the police and took my daughter from me. She then next rang up my publisher and taunted them with my arrest, and got my book deal canceled as furtherance of her willful efforts to crush me.

She went hard at me to try and have me trown in jail, crush my career, and see if she could make sure everything I had was ruined.

Oh how it worked. She got me fired from my job, got my assets seized by the UK police with a lie about me being involved with gangsters in London whom she claimed would use to kill her.

I was fucked so many ways from all of her efforts because she made sure to call and tell as many others as she could. It took a letter from my boss who ran the Charity that I worked for, (who had an "Order

of Excellence" from the Royal family) to use his influence for the credentials needed to have me released from custody.

Three days after I was arrested all of charges from my arrest were dismissed against me, but by that point I had already lost millions and millions of dollars.

Next Karen then used the family courts to get my rights to care for my daughter taken away from me. After hundreds of thousands of pounds spent by me for a legal battle for Lara over two years, I finally gave up on my daughter being allowed to be part of my life.

I can tell you in all honesty, having my career ruined, having my daughter then stolen from my life, and having my money stripped away to where I was basically screwed, all made me want so much to get my ass out of England.

First I went and lived alone in Holland. Then I tried to come back to England as Europe alone sucks.

I got a house in a place near Hastings England after I gave up on trying to live in places that I did not know anyone.

My friend Sulemon from Nigeria came and stayed at my house there while I filed a multi-million pound lawsuit against the publishers who had wrongfully canceled my first book due to what Karen did. Thousands of copies were sold of my book all over the world, and I was being eaten alive by all of these messages I got from readers.

In early 2010 I got tired of being praised for something that no longer existed to me and I went back to the USA. I went back to go get my brother Mikey and give he and I a chance at better. We flew first class to Las Vegas from Philadelphia and Mikey was smashed before the plane took off.

We were going to go to California so that we could look at land there that was for sale. The plan was that he and I would raise horses there as we get a chance then to get away from the shit in Philly that we had to go through.

I had a house back in England to sell to pay for this, so I was going to sell that place and get this land for us to live on. To hell with all of this speaking career, making movies, being a published author. All I could do then was file a lawsuit for the 60.000 copies which they dumped onto the market without paying me, and hope that I won.

Even though I would indeed win the lawsuit against Haper Collins UK for how I got screwed by them, it did not undo all the harm done to my career.

If not for all of the sorrow back in England that I was dealing with, my brother and I would have had an astounding time of fun and seeing things that blew us away. I drove to Hollywood after we visited the horse property for sale. I pulled up in front of his idol, the singer Mick Jaggers former house while were there. We smoked cigars and peed into the glass holders and put the caps back on before burying them in land where new houses were being built in Las Vgas. I even got Mikey laid by a professional call girl in Vegas.

When I parted ways with my brother I promised him that as soon I got the money we would go.

That was the last time I saw my brother alive again.

When I went back to the UK following my time with Mikey I tried to put my house up for sale on a shit market still suffering from the 2008 financial collapse.

It was then that I meet a girl named Jessie. Here it comes again, getting drawn towards love and what I really needed to feel inside so that everything what has been taken from me hurts less.

Losing my child to the courts, being driven mad by so much loss financially, against my wanting to get Mikey to safety... this was getting to be too much. I called my father and asked him what I should do.

My father said that he could take care of Mikey for now but that I needed to stay in England and try to sort my life out for Lara to be allowed back with me.

I told him how vicious Karen was being and he said I had a duty to stay.

I admit that I let him talk me out of what I should have done then, and it proved a really bleak truth to come because my brother Mikey died soon after.

Broke my own heart knowing that I chose to not keep my word to him, to take him with me away from Philly.

I was so fucking hurt inside because this was my guy, my friend, the one whom I was closet to in life.

At one point I went and got my brothers ashes from home and I brought them back to England with me. Mikey was a huge

Rolling Stones fan like I shared here, so I spread his ashes at the Mick Jagger Performing Arts School in Kent England. I did what I could for what I was

living down inside. Had I just taken him with me he would not have drunk himself to death.

   I hate me at times for letting go of what I swore he and I would go and do, my empty promise that we would both get out of that shit hole where we grew up.

  At this point I swear to God this last time here that the outside world was more cruel and crushing to me than all my years of being on Death Row.

  In there, the one defining difference is how you are singled out for attacks out of hate inside, while outside you are receiving the same level of aimed hurts for love.

   Every person whom I ever loved since being set free has gotten revenge upon me for that one act.

    Watch what I do as this just continues on at each of my life's junctures, regardless of my own efforts to find a love, or the things I did for it.

  Jessie? This will be the next one on my ex wives list that I am not "giving a whole lot of Oxygen to" as they say,.

  It is partly due to the fact that I am still close to her father in life, Chris. I am not trying to hurt my friend writing a great deal of nasty things about his child. But lets state how it went with this

incident also for clarity and cohesiveness to this story...

  Initially Jessica's family (Not with her dad involved) called the police to my house claiming that she was there against her will when their daughter left home to move in with me on her own accord.

    Then they plotted to plant heroin in my house and have me falsely arrested for drugs. Then, of course I had to move to where she lived and sell my house, get a normal job and please everyone for the next 3 years by showing everyone how I gave up speaking.

I thought getting a normal job, staying off of the stage and trying to have the most common life would work. I tried to have a family with Jessie, I made friends in Lincolnshire, I wrote an earlier version of this book, found out while doing so that I was making it all too ego driven, so I tossed it aside.

I didn't care that I was not chasing money, I was happy that the circus was not in town any longer, with my life being the main entertainment for everyone to laugh at.

And when it was good, when I was getting over the loss of Mikey dying, working through letting go of my own daughter, two really shitty things happened…

First one was my mother dies.

I was at work at my job in a town called Peterborough England working for the store chain named B&Q when I got a call to let me know my mother fell down a flight of steps and died shortly after.

She had Alzheimer's disease and forgotten how to walk down steps, so she fell down the steps at my father's feet with her last words in life upon landing were; "Help Me Mike, Help Me!"

I scraped together money, got on a last minute flight to New York City from England, and I went back to Philly in a huge rain storm in September 2011. It was treacherous to go to my father's house and attend my mother's funeral. Not just from the storm. With her gone, I had no buffer from my family now acting as vulgar as possible towards me.

One aspect of my life that is weird is that I have a profile with the Intelligence services. I had encounters with both the American Homeland security, as well as British intelligence.

That factor made it eerie that when I got off of a last

minute booked flight from London to NYC from Kuwait on the tenth anniversary of the 911 attacks in that city. However it was not a mind blowing thing for me to be taken out of line in immigration by TSA agents at JFK airport who then escorted me past customs, right to the rental cars counter. There they handed me my rental agreement to sign gave me my car keys, as they then
walked with me out of the terminal.

The TSA agents ended up at my rental car while telling that they were sorry for my loss. They and hoped that they had managed to make this part easier on me for me to go to my mother's funeral.

I stood there the whole time like a Death Row
prisoner, absorbing all told to me and not even making one comment. I didn't ask how the hell they knew I was on my way to my mother's funeral, nor how they knew which rental car counter to walk me over to.

None of it mattered I was just grateful they were not stopping me.

The roads were flooded in the area so it took me hours to get to my fathers house from New York City. It was late in the evening when eventually I got there.

I walked up to the door, opening the screen door to open the front storm door of the house, when I see Anna sitting right there in my mother's reclining chair through the glass. I opened both doors and entered.

No words, just the most disgusted snort which was aimed in my direction and then Anna turned to my father and said that she was leaving.

My father was so hurt by this cold as ice greeting when Anna and both had just lost our mother. I could see him deciding against challenging her.

I didn't feed into what Anna had done when she saw it was me, I told my father that I was sorry if my being there was going to ruin the funeral.

I even offered to go stay at a hotel and only come to the Wake.

No, my father said I was welcome to attend my mother's funeral, but that I was not allowed to speak afterwards.

I agreed to do whatever he wanted of me as I was not there for some need I had to "Do a talk" as it was said to me in taunts at times.

Both Anna and my oldest sister Nettie stood with their backs to me deliberately while we all stood in the receiving line of my own mother's funeral. No bullshit.

Mabel, my sister closest in age to me stood next to me, a gap separating us from Nettie and Anna who stood together to greet well wishers who passed by them after passing my mother's casket to where they stood.

"Sissy", as we called my sister Mabel growing up was looking at what was being done by the others. She took pity on me for what Nettie and Anna were doing in front of my mother's casket, so she stood next to me closer.

Sissy then introduced me to the ones whom I did not recognize as they came along, and everyone ignored how members of my own family were bullying me in front of my dead mother.

I endured this shameful act in front of my dead mother's body without ruining it for my father.

When all others passed by, I went and I knelt in front of my mother's casket. I swore on my knees that no matter what the others did to me, how I was going to be the promise of a man that she made me swear to her that I would become.

I placed a copy of my first book in her casket, then I kissed her one last time. No tears, no emotion, I could not hold my self together if I cracked then, I was too hurt by what had just been done to me in front of dozens of well wishers to cry.

I spoke for a few moments after everyone else did at her funeral, but my heart was not in it. I then finished my duty to my parents by attending the "Wake" where everyone started their drinking. I said all the polite goodbyes there and I got on my way to New York and get on a plane back to the UK.

I never wanted to not be me so much as I did that day in front of my own mother's casket. My sisters got me good. Whatever I did in any way that offended them, they got me back better than anyone could have that day. I kept thinking about my mother Jayne as I drove. All she wanted was for me to be a nice man. If I could pull off this request, and keep my mouth shut about how shitty it was to break my heart like this when my mother died..., then I was going to make her so proud of me I kept saying internally.

Not one drink, not one argument from me, I did everything my father asked of me. I then politely left as soon possible.

Once I got outside of Philadelphia I pulled over on the roadside and I cried finally for Jayne. She deserved better than her death being used as a cheap act of revenge from her daughters upon me.

I cannot imagine how she would feel knowing her own family was so dysfunctional.

While my mother was dying in the hospital her own family fought in the lobby of the hospital with tasers being pulled out after my father tossed the ones who came there high on drugs out.

It was the ones who were kicking off out of there for causing trouble and being doped up who stood with their back to me when my mother did die.

The hypocrisy to treat me as an outcast for not being held to their bullshit moral level burned big time for me emotionally.

I know that what was done to me was really payback for
how much my mother loved me, and that moreover because she had endeavored to prove my innocence to the point that they resented my being loved by her that much.

I also bore a second crime in their eyes of my knowing about all of the low things which they did while I
was in jail (that my mother told me about) made me see through them.

You see, while I was sitting in a cell I did not add to the family trauma.

That meant that I was not adding to things. I was not the one who damaged things with marital squabbles, drugs and drunken actions, as all the others continued on doing.

For my knowing all of that, they resented me deeply. Oh they hated how I was the 'agony aunt" with whom my mother shared all of their deeds with. And it is that knowing all their dirty secrets that drove them to hate me for trying to rise up and be better than that.

My mind was made up for me by their callous deeds that
day. I told my father that no matter what, I would never
stand in front of his casket while members of his family used his death for another payback upon me.

I told him as I left that I don't want anything from him, and that whatever he leaves behind, how I don't want any part of that either. I shook his hand like a fellow man before I left. I told Mike Yarris sr. that I was done.

In life, a whole lot of people understand it when I state
without reserve that I am glad that I shed my family like a bad mantle that was shackled to my neck.

I am not better than they are, I am not somehow a better human being than they are just because they hurt me personally.

I just became estranged from a pod of my species and I went on to make my own family without them. The message offered to me was clear. Go get away from the first version of you as a boy that they all hated when they knew you back then.

Go and embrace what I am entitled to, find a life without a ball and chain of lies that is tethering me to a family who feel some justified need to punish me.

They will always be excusing of all of their own bullshit in the process I know. I tell anyone in life how they should too should do this.

No way now that I was stupid enough to fall for that role that was being handed to me in life by a dysfunctional family.

Then as I said, the second bad thing happened to me. I got a serious spinal injury on my job here in England not long after my mother passed away. Now without being entitled to benefits as I only have an indefinite Visa for me to remain in the UK, I was screwed financially.

Jessie worked in a pub tending bar, but we had to think about selling the house at some point. I was suffering from the T-1 and C-6 Spinal discs in my back both being shattered. along with trapped nerves in my chest and arm driving me mad with pain levels like few I ever had known before.

Then shit really got ruined for me even further from this injury, and just like all the nose dives before then, this one was really hard to handle…

Jessie and I had to leave England in 2013 after a horrible incident involving a couple who were friends of mine.It was either go to jail for want to hurt them, or deciding on going to America and seeking a chance for my film rights to come about as a major motion picture.

That appealed more to me than going to jail for what was being done to my partner when I walked into a room and they were all drunk…

America. Los Angeles…it's too big. It is too much and too big as there are simply too many men are there very with similar stories from Death Row for me to really stand out.

I am being brutally honest. I have a story, but over there in La La land, there are hundreds and hundreds men and women with the same story.

I was lucky I did not lose my life rights for all the many scammers thatI met there during this time. I put in a year of efforts trying to reprint my first book, set up speaking, or get a film made about my life.

Then Jessie walks in after year and some weeks later and tells me she is leaving me now that she has a life here in America.

Just like that she had a new man she was falling in love with and that is it.

I took this happening to me like a weakling I was truly crumbled. Sitting at a table in our kitchen in America she said to me that one day I would end up like "The Dancing Man", some poor guy back in Lincolnshire who lost it mentally when his wife left him. She said my acting all devastated made her sure I would end up like he did.

That was her telling me to stop crying about her leaving me when I truly loved her.

I burned our mementos in the fireplace we had in our house in located in Claremont California, and left.

Moving on I went and I got my two dogs and myself settled into an American RV that I bought cheaply. Then I got out of Los Angeles as soon as I was able to.

After all that I did for Jessie…Trips to Vegas, Surpise Honeymmon in Hawaii, all of the fancy dinner nights in Los Angeles with her…they don't mean shit when you can have it all with someone else. You get to forget about what happened just before we left England and go be some new version of you.

Because that way booze parties don't lead to
shit happening that ruins everything back there. No this way here those things lead to new friends, and a new guy who drinks booze just like you do.

The revenge Jessica got on me was not some aimed cruel act. Hers was making me feel ugly and old.

Being left by her because of my age was as hurtful as
stealing my child before I met and married Jessie. I spent nearly 100.000 dollars trying for a baby with her. It felt like once that was not to be for us, a flip of switch took place in her head.

Suddenly it was singles clubs and the party girl took over. Soon enough she was convinced that I was basically in her way of her new life.

This event hurt as much as someone making sure my
parents would not welcome my new wife because she was with a black man. It made me think anyone else was going to see me as old and unattractive like this.

Then I hurt myself to the point of boils appearing on my flesh as I tried hard to punish myself for loving her so deeply.

I did Jessie, I loved you so very much honey. I
am sorry for my reactions to your leaving me that were cheap and petty, but I was so betrayed by you, and so hurt for the loss of 6 years with you that I hated myself for how you made me feel.

It took me years to be able to even say your name and not feel awful inside. It is what it is, and what happened after you left my life made it of course worse on me. Whatever hurtful feelings I caused you got re-payed upon me big time if that helps of matters.

If there is one gift that Jessie gave to me, it is how I finally accepted my age. Don't matter if I have ultra young body, I was

54 years old, she was 27 then.

Its all gone now, and I got done with doing the mental battles of how it played out, when things showed me how badly they could really go from this point.

I learned the real lesson about how the way we chase money is much like how we chase love, swearing in each instance how we cherish what it brings to us.

I was still willing to believe that I could find love with someone long term. I still had a sweetness about me that someone would love to have aimed at them. I just did not want to believe all of this was my fault. That I wrecked things because I am somehow cursed to have this life.

What happens next after I got dumped by Jessie?

I go from my mother dying and the worst funeral experience possible, to my wife leaving me for a younger man, to then millions and millions of people globally suddenly think that I am the most desirable man whom they could ever imagine as loving them...

Just like that. One month I was on the streets living in the RV, and then the next one, I am suddenly globally recognized from the film The Fear Of 13 being released.

This set off a wild ride that all unfolded while I was homeless and living out of a RV in California. You cannot make this up.

I woke up one morning and my phone would not stop giving me notifications of messages literally all day. Notifications of over 100.000 messages just shuts down a phone eventually.

That was the most insane onslaught of attention that I had ever gotten in life to that point.

Netflix released my film globally and all hell broke loose, hundreds of thousands of people tried to contact me on Facebook, and or my second website which I had back then, as well as platform once known asTwitter.

Women of ever walk of life saw that I was single at the time online and I had hundreds of offers to "Come visit" this one or that one.

I went from being made to feel tired and old and being dumped for my being at this point of my life, to then being hit with endless offers from women who fell in love with me from watching this film.

I was not as silly as in the past, but yeah, I indulged. I got all kinds of revenge on all my past lovers and I was a total dog about it no doubt.

I was seeing a couple of women in Los Angeles, the land of soon to be actresses who are stunning and fun to be with to forget about anything else.

This was wildly different than my being some bum on the road that just got dumped, I had my pick of ladies for months if I wanted to.

"All hell broke loose part 2", is what I like to call what then happened next then, because the BBC channel showed my movie in England on national television two consecutive nights in a row..

The audiences went wild for this film back in the UK. Instantly I was paid to fly back to London and sell my rights for a new TV series to be made called Dead Man Talking... I next got offered to have a stage play developed, as well as a new book deal from a second major publisher.

Just like that, all soaring upwards for me with millions for me on the table. To this point I still had no flinch about me,. I was going to believe in all of this new good despite being a two time loser to this point. It takes a lot to be Nick Yarris is my own internal mantra that I at times have to pull out and use.

This next part is going to prove this with aplomb. As I sit before this keyboard with the enormity of what I have had to deal with since my release, it feels so unreal. It is so much like something that I have to actually write in order to accept it as I go forward.

Otherwise, and I mean this when I say it, that without the right mindset, how this one book might be the onus of my snapping he fuck out in anger for all of the absolute shit that I have had thrown in my face.

Seriously, because I keep having the temerity, or the the gumption to want to be loved and be in love, that is my crime for which I have to be so severely punished?

A lesser man picks up a gun and seeks vengeance. Me? I simply wanted to achieve enough money to get my daughter Lara back in my life, to then start over with my hopes of being a father to her. I wanted to be a family man despite all this wasted time on others so far.

Kind of weird that at one point I was all sad for being drubbed over getting dumped, to then being all cavalier about being with new women.

Obviously I was functioning on a high level of stress as is reflected by so much going on. I was going through all of this in a bravado driven facade that had many layers of hurt that never got resolved hidden within it all.

From the shitty reason why I went to Los Angeles with Jessie, on through to why I had to get out of there later, this is just how it all went.

I went from being a millionaire with all this bright sunlit driven effort, to feeling what it was like to lose it all like it was blown from your hands in some huge wind storm. I found out who my real friends were when we shared tears, or they saw me as someone odd. All I was doing was trying my best to still find some life not blown to bits by yesterday.

CHAPTER FOUR: DREAMS KEPT COMING, NO MATTER WHAT

I left my dogs named Pokey and Delilah whom I shared with Jessie to be with my friend Tyler in Utah. I left my RV in Los Angeles with a guy who was supposed to stay in it there until I came back, and then I went back to England on a flight that had "The Fear Of 13" on the in-flight

entertainment system.

Photos with staff on board when I woke up, passengers cannot believe it is me, and the lead producer of the morning TV show in England is seated next to me. This is too corny to contrive.

I got off of the flight like a celebrity, got my ass up to Peterborough, where my friend Marcin Puchowski hands me keys to a car.

Then Marcin hands me UK cash and gets me a

place to stay in the Eastern European community there in the city. I then went to work trying to sell my writing projects while I drove around England, just trying to decide how to try to make this comeback work.

Yes, got my first book re-published under the title "The Fear of 13, My countdown to Execution"...lame.

I got speaking gigs set up, and I drove my little free car from Marcin all over England, indulging in my single lifestyle with not one bit of guilt about it. I wasn't cheaply arrogant, I just said yes a whole lot for a warm bed and food and then I went my way afterwards.

Then I meet Laura. Honestly I was okay with a cute normal looking girl that she was. I did not need to cater to the "I am hot, I have power" of a prissy girl type.

We had such a connection right off that I didn't care that she had two little girls.

I was so into her, that I quit messing around and stayed at her place located in a tiny village out near Stonehenge England while I wrote a new book that I titled "Monsters and Madmen".

I found out Laura was actually still pregnant from her previous partner, and still I stayed with her. I helped her bring a beautiful child into this world named Jaymie Leigh, named in honor of my mother.

With Random House publishers helping me, I was back on British TV, I was back on stage to standing ovations, while I was in love with Laura. I loved her babies, I used her love to ascended the heights to the point that I was invited to Geneva. It was where my film was to be shown before the Human Rights Counsel who then heard me speak so beautifully after the film.

I strolled around Lake Geneva with Laura and the baby in the pram like I owned the world that night.

***There is such a need right here to share something. I have to pause right here because this night in Geneva was the happiest day of my life as a free man.

There were two huge converging factors driving this. The first was how Laura was shown in real time how women with careers, women who had high status envied her for being on my arm. The way she was treated with deference was like nothing she had ever had aimed at her in life. I kept telling her how she could now see that she was as equal and deserving of being in any social setting that there was. It made Laura have such a profound perspective of herself.

The second came part of this was how I so loved her that as we walked around Lake Geneva with the baby, I stopped with her before a huge Oak tree and we swore our vows of mariage before that tree.

I said that trees are the longest witness of humans, I then said that as long as this tree was here how I would love her and my words to her. I know this hurts, but I had to say again how much I loved this one woman.

Back in the UK while living with Laura, I even got a major motion picture deal offered to me. It actually all happened because of Muhammad Ali of all humans. I got a call from Los Angeles from Anthony Samadani, a man who once shared Friday prayers with this historic figure of a man that Ali was.

That was the day by coincidence that the US patent office for it's first time in history granted patent rights to someone within one working week. It was granted to the Muhammad Ali foundation for the bracelet bearing the words "Within Good, There IS God".

My first phone call with Anthony Samadani began with a quest he had for me. He asked me what gave me my spirituality.

Without hesitation, I told Anthony how my mother told me that all she ever prayed for was "Good", and that she had told me that is what any human who prays to God should ask for.

Anthony was so struck by this that he then told me that just that very day the US Patent Office had just done something that it never had done previously.

That is when I knew I would give my life rights to this man. In the years since we met and had that phone call in 2016, Anthony has witnessed every aspect of this journey I made since.

Once I had Anthony love me and want to help me inside I felt as I was going to take Laura and just shine for the world. Here I am world, no matter what has been done previously, I am here!

Living with Laura, Bethany, Zara, and newborn Jaymie Leigh was probably the best days that I had on some levels. Taking the family into London and being put up in the penthouse of the Crown Plaza hotel while I went on TV, going to book festivals, and always laughing.

Marcin and his wife Joanna were so in love with the baby, Marcin was so relieved that I was happy, even my father was happy that I was not off drifting about.

The coolest part was when the children's grandmother Marie would take them to her house so Laura and I got to go all over Europe promoting my book for Random House publishers.

We were like two teenagers who had been sent on holiday for the way we loved Germany, could not believe how fun Wales was, and the sweetest one was going to Ireland and visiting the Trinity Colleges, home to hundreds of my favourite authors. Laura and I found the same kind of beautiful Oak tress on the grounds of this impressive institution. I had a moment with Laura at the base of this one tree where I told her that no matter what, no matter how things went, I wanted to come back to this spot.

I still had some of my brother Mikey's ashes in a glassine packet tucket into my wallet. I had been carrying that around since his death.

I left the last bit of his remains there and did not say a word that I did so. I just dug it out on the sly and left it there.

Still, that first year with Laura was magical for her and I both. What a romance we shared!

Then comes the most cruel, the worst of shit of all…

January 2017.

I convince Laura to lie down with me on the downstairs sofa in our flat in Illchester when she has Flu. She was cleaning too much and wearing herself thin.

We lie together on her sofa for no more than 20 to 30 minutes. I get up to go check on Jaymie Leigh in her crib, and she is dead.

I scream in horror as I run downstairs with the baby in my arms.

Did I not tell you?

Don't you see what I had alluded to all along, how no matter what, I am so besot with huge misfortunes one after another, all by my own life's path? My life is filled with things that I have no control over, so what am I to do?

I wish I could make any of this up, yet a lot of folks think that I have to somehow lie, because no life could ever be this twisted and shot through with pain.

The sinister always need to try to be evil. That is what happened next…

Karen, or one of the ones whom she recruits online to crowd stalk me for years now contacted the police about
a "Tweet" that I posted online the day that Jaymie Leigh died.

It was a pious message to cherish whom we love in life. That's all it took for me to be tormented online and in life.

The "time stamp" of my post was off from UK time because my phone being left on California time.

That little "thing" gave my stalkers a chance to hurt me, and especially Laura by contacting the police and telling them that I had posted something online right when the baby died, so isn't that proof he killed the baby?

The police asked me about this in front of Laura after they had lied to us that day on the phone as they said that they had "information about the baby's death".

The police came to our flat and they asked me why my "Tweet" was posted near to the time of death of the baby, only for me to not say a word.

As Laura screamed at them in horror for this cruel thing, I stood still looking at this officer for a long moment. How fucked up to insinuate I was somehow involved in killing a baby as I lay with Laura on her sofa.

What a low thing to have done to us after we were so desperate for news of what happened to the baby.

I simply said nothing this whole time as I walked with a UK police officer into the kitchen, and I asked them to have a look at my phone sitting there. Pick the phone up and see that it is set to 8 hours off for being still on California time I told them.

I explained that my phone time was done this way as my friend Anthony Samadani was working on my movie deal back in Los Angeles where I had just moved from.

Still, knowing that my stalker was hurting Laura by default, messing with me on top was a shitty act for anyone to pull when a child dies.

In the aftermath of what was ruled a SIDS death, I literally for years suppressed my grief. Laura came first in my heart, she could never be usurped by my making this about me, or my sad saga of a life.

So I ate all of the pain, nightmares, or the crushing remembrances of that day when I picked Jaymie Leigh up. It hurt, I did not have any ability to stop being furious that someone hurt us as a couple by making out I killed this beautiful child whoom I so adored.

I hurt myself suppressing it all to the point that I had all sorts of nightmares. Cruelly the same scenario of finding Jaymie dead with no ability of mine to pick her up as m arms never work in my dreams. I feel myself screaming for help that never comes for me.

After this cheap act with the police from my online stalkers, I got Laura and her two girls out of the flat where the bay died, and everything fell apart for us.

I went back to America for my film to be made with Laura agreeing that this was best for us all.

I wanted to have all of these big time chances offered to me about this movie deal to get us to that next level.

I thought to myself okay; "Maybe this time I will get the biggest upswing ever, and then I can leave all of this pain and sorrow behind me finally"...

I sat down then and I wrote a new book that I titled "The Approach" after this horrible event with a SIDS
death.

My inspiration for the book came as I was sitting on a
wall in a village in Southwestern England.

I was sitting on a wall one sunny day in early 2017 after a walk to just get out of the flat. I was facing a field across from a river that once kept the locals from entering town. Illchester England was once a Roman prison town at one point. Cross that river and die prisoner.

And as I sat there with an eerie feeling that I some how just knew inside for all the world that I had seen that one lone image in my head, long before I sat here that day for sure.

It was all so real to me that this image which I saw then had to captured on a phone camera which I had with me. It would be this image that became the one on the book front exterior.

I sat one day and thought all about what I had been
through just before I left that place.

Now having written that book, one that to this day was my effort to step away from just prison related writings, I was proud that my was my answer to the biggest loss of my life. No bitterness, no outbursts, I had the biggest humbling of my life and instead of being a nasty, empty hearted man, I offered the world a chance to find Neuro

healing of the mind. It takes nothing to indulge bitterness. Easy for some to just feel that tightness in your jaws as your mind feeds off of your own poison.

Jaymie Leigh Yarris deserved better than that type of conduct or behaviour from me, I honestly believe that as I went forward without being broken inside.

I thought maybe this new offer of a movie deal, (along with connections from powerful people from

my film being on Netflix),as well as a change of scenery would fix all of this sorrow.

Laura took the loss of this precious child

hard. The two girls lost their baby sister, and I was

swallowing a huge PTSD ball of pain so that they could all

escape without me ruining it.

In June of 2017, I left England with Laura and her two

daughters and we flew to California once again in my life.

We took the girls to Disneyland and began to erase all of the trauma of the death in our little clan.

While in Los Angeles I went to work to have a script

written about my life story and had director Alejandro

Monteverde agree to make a motion picture about my

journey. I married Laura on the Beach in Playa Del Vista

beach with the girls in attendance. Anthony Samadani performed the ceremony on the beach and it felt like all of our hurts and pain were a million miles behind us all.

It started to look like this plan was perfect, but these dreams kept coming to me, telling me that I was not to

rest. Other ones also jumped out vividly as well...

What I am bout to next share still to this day makes me both utterly grateful others witnessed this all, as well as totally disheartened for how it was an onset of woes for me which I never dreamed possible.

I was sitting in a meeting in Los Angeles with three men who had proposed to me that I join a Podcast that needed a new co-lead to revitalize it.

Laura was with the two children at a park next to where we had left our rental car just a few blocks away.

That meeting in which the man John said something to me about what car we were driving, and suddenly that was when I got hit by the most powerful image of a blonde haired girl huddled in a car in pain. That image was from no dream that I ever had since release. I could tell you the cell number that I was on L-block in Greene County Supermax prison, I could tell you how I never even thought about that since having the dream, why would I?

Yet, as I sat there in Los Angeles talking to these men, I saw plain as day in my mind that dream which I had of which that image was so clearly the oldest daughter of Laura's named Bethany who in pain. Just like in a dream I once had long before then of that blonde child hurt and I had to run to her, that is how I would find her soon.

Right in front of these three men, I stood up from the table and said how I have to go outside to make a phone call to my wife, one of her children is in trouble. I never had my phone out, I was in the middle of a sentence about what car we drove when all of this flashed into my brain.

With the others outside with me, my hands now were shaking

while holding my phone, I stood on the street with my heart racing wildly as I waited to hear Laura connect to me.

Laura answered me right away and she was all upset as she explaining to me that she was tending to her injured daughter who in the back seat of the car and she would not let Laura see her arm.

The three men from the meeting came with me to the park were Laura was on foot., they then went with me by car to a local emergency care unit.

These men I hardly knew paid for Beth to go to this Emergency clinic first , but that was before we all soon

realized that this was too serious of an injury. We took her to Cedars Sinai Hospital in Los Angeles that was located nearby.

It was there where they performed micro-surgery, with the only qualified surgeons available in the area, all high end amazing surgery that ended up costing 76.000 dollars.

We had no health care insurance to pay for all of this. I gave the hospital as much as I could. I then paid for all of the post operation treatments out of pocket as well. Then we took some of the remaining money that I was paid for my life story rights to buy a big Motor-home.

With all the first episode in Los Angeles unfolding for us so badly, we took off up and down the west coast of America, hoping to try and just let time play out.

I had three months there to drive to Canada and do a huge event in Calgary for big money that I was to be paid to speaking before it's 2000 employees. That money would cover the loss of the medical bills, buying the RV and let us go back to England with money.

I was so shook for one of my long ago dreams coming true with my seeing that child getting hurt in a dream long before now, that I just kept feeling this omnipresent cloud over me because of it.

No matter what. run, move, hide, this cloud of pain kept doggedly climbing over any barrier to press down on me.

I prayed so hard to let it all stop, let these little girls have some good is all I wanted.

Look, all the magic in the world cannot stop pain for long. I know that. But being on the road can be so good to not have you sit and think of the really harsh reality that you have to endure. I felt my wife cry so many nights in her sleep that I never thought she could be as amazing as she was during the day.

My mind was set on trying anything that I could to help this woman who came to a new country after losing a baby in so cruel of a manner, then just had her oldest daughter break her elbow.

So, change...just make it chance Nicky. So I did. I got Laura new boobs, new puppies we bought in a park by a Chinese couple using Facebook, bought them all new clothes and we set off for a new life.

I gave us all a new chance to erase all the shit we both Laura and I had to go through, with so many unfair things happening us so unfairly.

It was going to have to be our healing, or another complete ruination. If it is not obvious by now, it was the second one of these two things for me in this story. I wish with all my heart I could just flip past this next bit,

but so be it...

CHAPTER FIVE: WE ALL PROCESS GRIEF DIFFERENTLY.

I am not allowed into Canada. The so called "Reciprocal Law" that exists between Canada and the USA is so petty that anyone convicted in a crime in either country can be denied entry.

It does not matter that I was set free from Death Row by DNA, Canada is caught up in a petty boarder battle with America and I had to pay a huge financial loss for this.

I went on a three month journey with Laura and her girls all over California in that RV. The children loved waking up in new places while seeing some of the best childhood things that one could possibly witness.

Honestly this was a magical time to erase all the trauma from which we all suffered.

America can be a floating dream at times, where you can park your RV and have anything you want delivered to the very spot that you parked your vehicle.

Laura had so much of a revival during these months, feeling confident with her body, she was enjoying the many activities with me and the children that we just relished. Water parks, the Ocean, Big Bear lake. It was just all so amazing for two girls under the age of 7 and their mummy to discover.

Trust me I saw then how was crushing it was for Laura when it all seemed to end right at the Canadian boarder.

I was sitting in a camp site in Washington State, just near the Boarder with Canada. I was facing a huge choice.

I spent so much money getting there that I was stuck way out there on a limb. I was on the hook for all of my expenses now that I could not make it to Calgary.

We had swapped out the RV (Which we left parked on the streets there) for a SUV. We then fitted the SUV with a 6X4 cargo trailer. We used this set up to tow my 2.000 copies of my hardback books inside of to this event in Canada.

I went on Facebook marketplace ads looking for some form of housing we could use. Laura had had enough of all this madness by then and she needed some place to heal.

I saw a place in Oregon that looked too good to be true. Over 4 acres of Land on a mountain side just next to the Pacific ocean in southern Oregon. That was some 390 miles south of where I sat.

I then saw that this fully furnished house down in southern Oregon was available immediately so I showed it to Laura.

My wife loved it when we drove up the coast of both Northern California, all the way to Washington state as we drove through Oregon.

I called the person who was using the add online, and the next day I drove all the back to the California boarder in one shot.

Just like that and we moved into a huge 4 bedroom house set on 4 beautiful acres of land that overlooking a pacific mountain named Mount Milan...I cannot make that up.

The house belonged to rich couple who had retired early, only to not like the quiet of the small community there, so they rented it out.

I went to work doing speaking, I got the children enrolled in school, and then I let Laura heal in this paradise which had humming birds, a lemon tree out front, and deer who calmly romped in the back garden. Every day we went with the children to the beach, Laura and her two Puppies always leading the way. This really helped despite losing so much money.

By the summer of 2018 I was healed enough with my spinal chord injury to go to work building houses. I stayed away from the multi-million dollar pot industry because everyone doing it also was involved in crime most of the time and no way I wanted that trouble. I had my friend Donnie get me work doing house framing.

We barely hung on a lot of the times, the house bills were a lot to cover financially, so Laura tried to start her own cleaning business. It was slow going and we began to feel all the stress of not having resources as we did before the mishaps befell us.

I decided to chase after things by going on the Joe Rogan podcast. I knew that if I did this, I would really energize my chances there in America. I swear, how it all went down is a real twisted series of events though.

I had an offer to be the face for a new educational platform from a guy from New Zealand, then living in America, who had offered me 200.000 per year job to get this project funded.

I flew to Las Vegas at one point and I got a meeting over the line, to where the investor said yes to putting up millions of dollars, only for the investor to change his mind, later.

I told this guy about being on the Joe Rogan podcast and he said he had a plan to get us the investment we needed.

Meanwhile, all of this happened to begin with because Joe Rogan is born the same day as Jaymie Leigh was who died the previous year.

On the platform once called Twitter my one time

friend Brian back in England tweets out all this praise for his hero Joe Rogan on his birthday.

I thought about how Joe Tweeted in 2016 about he and I doing a podcast episode on his platform with a huge "LET'S DO THIS!",…only for me to not hear from this man, despite trying for years to catch up with him.

So, online on the post about his birthday, I told Brian to fall back, and that "dude was not like that".

Then I got a direct message from Joe on Twitter saying he would put me on his show.

I then had only contact with his staff setting up my flight to Burbank to do his show, did not know if he was angry at me for what I wrote, I just was very polite to his staff in my emails.

I met this man 5 minutes before I went on air. I took a photograph with him and Anthony Samadani, and then I put on headphones and sat down.

Oh man, what happened in between that Tweet that led to me there in that chair and and me meeting Joe for his podcast was straight out of Hollywood itself.

I mean it. When your first action you decide to do for being on the biggest podcast in the USA is to see your chest area for a T-Shirt, one for a company that makes protective sleeves for bottled Booze, you can see the red lights of signs flashing danger ahead.

Not then though, I just needed to keep the house going.

Laura had made friends in town, some who drank and did drugs and Laura starting drinking.

I was fighting with her about it, I was so tired of how alcohol was always a problem.

As I left to go to Joe's event I was sending all these argument laced phone messages back and forth to Laura while she was off on a trip in Oregon with her girlfriend.

My wife did not want me to meet anyone whom I had ever knew in Los Angeles, worried I would sleep with them, and I did not want her drinking like she was, nor doing my head in with paranoid beliefs.

I went to Los Angeles fuming that things were so soured between, when I had too much on my plate to think that way behind her back...

Then this guy from New Zealand, the one who told me he had a "brilliant plan" explained to me that he sent my

film link for Fear Of 13 to Oprah Winfery's husband Steadman Graham.

And...get this, that 3 million dollars that we needed?

We are getting ten times that amount now!

My man said to me by phone how this billionaire wanted me to meet him on the evening before the Joe Rogan podcast because he was so impressed by me.

In a blazing series of events, it went this way...

I fly to Burbank California from a trip that began at 5:30 am in Crescent City California Airport, to then fly to Oakland California, where by 5;30pm I finish my trip of flights. I check into my hotel in Burbank Joe paid for, I immediately get into a car, where I am driven at 80 miles per hour or faster to get down to Orange county.

My Buddy from New Zealand was my driver who was all hyper fast talking, with all this positive news about how we were going to this meeting with all these others, and how I was going to be the one they all needed to hear. I was told 40 influencers, and business people were dying to hear me speak.

Well yeah, that was all bullshit I would soon find out in a very shoddy manner.

I was focused on a meeting that has this man Steadman Graham center stage for me to speak to. I know I am going to smash this!

When I go down there listening to how Mr. Steadman's personal assistant has relayed all the many gracious things that this man has said about me, how could I not buy into all of this amazing good?.

I get to the event and in my best "You know me buddy" of an introduction, I come to find out that this man has no fucking clue who I am.

Seriously.

What a crazy set up. I guess my man did not think that I was going to out him right off, but telling Steadman so sincerely a thank you for saying how amazing my accomplishments were.

I was so stunned when this man's reaction was to ask me who I was, and how did I come to be there made my heart sink. I excused myself in utter humiliation as I stepped aside. I went and sat on one these many assembled chairs that were arranged in a circle totally stunned by what had just happened.

I told my guy from New Zrealand that I needed a minute. I was torn as to how to deal with this man who so deftly played me for an idiot.

And as I was about to walk out, They made everyone standand each person had two minutes to introduce themselves gathered on the other chairs....

Okay, so the set up was an assembled set of chairs with a host who came on stage, told everyone to sit, then began telling all how this was a gathering of investors and influencers in the fields of education, tech, and development of social programs.

Then the host of the event announced how each person had to stand up from there chair in order or right to left, with each person being given only 3 minutes of time. Each person had to tell the gathering who they are, what they did as an occupation, and what brought them to that chair.

Of all the times to have the near overwhelming urge to be a

total prick, and just say unreversable things, while surely make a fool of myself for letting my ego urge me to an outburst for being duped... THIS was that time.

Not NIck Yarris. I was not going to do that dumb kind of action. Thankfully I was lucky enough to be the 3rd or 4th person to have to stand up and speak within the three things they were allowed time to state.

Having got my shit together mentally by the time it came around to me, I dropped jaws open.

I hit them with what I had to say about who I was, I then segued perfectly into my work as an Author because of who I was, then finishing well short of 3 minutes, I said that before that moment of my speaking to them that I had no clue why I of all people would be here. I simply said I was brought by an associate right after I had gotten off of a flight just a few hours before then, so yes excuse me I have nothing to offer you all.

That was the most honest thing I could do by then.

The host waited for all of the other guests to finish speaking and he halted the process while announcing that he had to stop.

Then the host said that in all of the times he has ever been part of a gathering where others introduced themself, he had never been so blown away as he was right then. He got an Elder from a native American tribe who spoke about indigenous development who was a healer to stand up out of her chair. He made me stand up and come before the host with this woman on my right side, next to us both as we three faced the group.

They performed a ceremonial ritual blessing for me in front of everyone and it began to break my heart. I could not take it that I was receiving all of this attention while I was so full of sorrow.

For the first time ever I broke down on stage.

Finally, the overwhelming accumulation of sorrow and pain got to me. The way I was so humiliated just burned into me. I could not take another second of all this against a facade of a set up.

With tears flowing I explained that I had been brought there under the assumption that I was know by the main guest that was there, and that when I became aware of how I was mislead in thinking this hugely important man knew me, how I made a fool of myself. I then pathetically begged my leave, and walked out to them all in disbelief.

I sat in the parking area alone outside of that event looking at all the messages from Laura, wondering how the fuck can I explain to her I just blew it in front of anyone who could have helped us?

I honestly wanted to go home. Fuck the podcast, fuck going to movie meetings in the morning (that are all now so important now because I am doing this podcast), so hey, "we can get movie money"...Wow. Just wow.

I had less than 200 dollars on me, I had to go 70 miles to go back to my hotel as it is now 8:pm, so even if I left then, I was 3 hours in transit.

It must have been a good hour or so later and then that is when my man from New Zealand comes bouncing out of the place to find me leaning on the front of his car.

Honest moment: NO! I could not punch or beat this man because California is not any place you want to do time. Seriously. This guy was aware of what I had gone through to walk up to Steaman.

No, I gave my buddy that look which conveys to someone how they should keep their mother fucking mouths shut. The eyes that make plain that you fucked up so badly with me that your best and safest bet, is to play mute.

I asked bluntly: "You finished"? Followed immediately by; "Because I fucking am, now get in the car and get me to my hotel room and don't say a fucking thing to me, do you hear me?"

A timid guilty nod from his head said enough for me to keep composure, so get out of there Nicky and do not say anything!

I was driven in near complete silence back to Burbank that night. I told the man driving that I could not promise him that I was going to be able to refrain from breaking his face with my elbows for what he just did to me when he briefly tried to put this all on the Steadman's personal assistant, but that lie did not make sense. I told him to shut the fuck up one last time and to get me back to my hotel, and to not ever speak to me again.

Got to my hotel and the room about 11:pm and my hotel room phone had 20 missed calls...

The room has sealed windows, the bed has a goose down comforter instead of a blanket, and I'm so twisted up in all this sheer madness, that I cannot sleep.

All night angry texts with Laura who thinks I am in Los Angeles fucking someone behind her back, all night replaying the meeting melt down and how I cried in front of 40 people. I was so miserable.

Wake up the next morning from fitful one hour sleep near dawn and I go to a breakfast meeting with investors for the film deal. I cannot talk to anyone about all of this chicanery from the evening before.

Then that was followed by another meeting with the folks who wanted to go to the podcast along with me, so we get me ready to promote the booze cooler T-shirt. I go in studio shake Joe's hand, pose for a single photograph with him and my guy Anthony in it, and then I sat in the guest chair on the podcast set.

Honestly I was holding my shit together. As it began I said to Joe Rogan that now that the energy between us was better, we could do this.

That was me referring to how he blew me off, I got snippy about it online and called him out, and he tossed me this bone to help me out. Done.

I did the most shit job ever of being composed and then sharing my beautiful story after 15 minutes. I lost it.

All the many hours spent thinking how I was going to present this effort so beautifully, only for it all to turn to shit.

I was so humilated thinking that it took Jaymie Leigh dying in my arms from this fucking SIDS crap, only for me to have to have that be the onus for me to then sit before this man, wearing a stupid advertisment for booze bottles.

Now everyone can now know why I was such a wreck emotionally when I tried to do a podcast to help share with the world as much of a beautiful message as I could be proud of offering.

The only thing that really made all of this palatable to me, was the first of many messages which I got from the listeners to this Podcast.

The first man was a disabled Native American combat veteran who lost both legs in war, the next man who wrote me had told me how he had open heart surgery and got addicted to pain medication.

I mean, I could not even get my books sold properly because Random House publishers canceled my book
"Count Down To Execution" because previously in a Tweet I asked the for expanded distribution of my book
to America.

Don't ever talk shit about what you want to powerful on social platforms is the lesson that I learned, they will crush you quick.

Soon after that debacle I quit posting on Twitter.

The podcast got my speaking career a jolt for a short while.

Laura and I got our act together and kept going in strong back in Oregon, While my years long efforts to help Walter Ogrod get off of Deat Row like I promised him I would just got a bunch of major help.

All it took was being being the only man ever to turn down television station CNN, specifically their program "Death Row Stories"...Narrated by Academy Award Winner Susan Suranden.

I asked them to ignore me when I was asked to be on this show, I begged them help Walter instead. I then put

them in touch with the author named Tom Lowenstien whom I asked back when I was still on Death Row to write a book about Walter, and ignore me.

That's right, both on Death Row and here on the streets I am the kind of man who will give up his own chances for big things, so that another man gets his only hopes and prayers met. Not by God, but their prayers for me to come back for them were met.

That will always be me, even when I could have taken chances that would have been huge after this one here, I gave them up for my promise to others.

The promise I gave to Walter caused me to badly suffer a condition known as"survivors guilt" just for being free.

Can you grasp that? I would get so down while I imagined Walter on Death Row knowing in my heart that he was innocent.

The whole time that I was free this feeling never stopped bothering me. I always felt like I would see him

again somehow out here. That's all I knew to believe in.

In early 2020 as the COVD pandemic hit the world, all at the same time as DNA results proved Walter did not kill the little girl. I thought he was going to die in there from this desease sweeping the US prison systems.

I tried to go there to Philadelphia and see him in February of 2020 alone by car, but they shut down the whole world right then. I was not even sure, as I turned back from the state of Wyoming, having crossed half of north America by that point, if my friend would live through this series of delays of his freedom being granted.

Not only did I not go see Walter, but worse still, I lost all of my income right at that moment.

I was set to go back to Europe for a massive speaking tour, only to lose everything from this shut down of the globe. I literally lost 25.000 dollars overnight.

We had also moved closer to town, down from the expensive house on the mountain we were at, into a small run-down house by this time. Our landlord was a nasty drunkard. At 81 years old, while wearing a politically based red cap, (with an open carry pistol) began threatening us for the rent. He did not care about the Pandemic because Fox news said it was all fake.

In the course of a week he kept coming there and being a menace. The police said that as I lived on a public street he could drive past or walk by as much as he wanted until we went to court, which was of course shut down.

I chose not to take his gun off of him and beat his shaky old ass, or worse be shot by him in front of the children, so we borrowed a trailer off of some folks in town and we moved into the national forest.

Laura and I started off on the banks of the Chetco river living in a tent next to the children who had the protection inside the small trailer from elements we dealt with, like our cat named Marmite bringing a BAT that he caught into the tent and it flying wildy around us, or the Mountain Lions who screams at night are next level. This was not some vacation, this went on for month and months into summer with all the night time druggies and drunks coming there to party on the river banks.

We dealt with bears, drunken brawls on the river, (Beth broke her arm again...)we had marauders try to raid us in the night only for me to come out of the tent with a huge Machette and chased them off... and endless guns. Just always people firing guns in the woods.

By the rainy season we had met two other sets of campers living like we were so we formed a group and moved off the banks of the river, deeper into the woods.

We found a clearing big enough to park several motorhomes and cars, with a fire cut road leading out. It was called Snaketooth ridge on the maps. What a crazy thing to have to do experience with three dogs a cat and 4 others.

The two other men with me helped clear the road from fallen trees, we built make shift structures down at the pad we were going to live on and then we got the vehicles all arranged in a circle at set up power sharing from my generator.

I stayed in the clearing of our camp most days while Laura drove into town and cleaned houses. I kept the children in school online from the top of the mountain, at a location that got reception…and we just kept going. Maybe God protected us all keeping us hidden in the woods like that while this pandemic raged across the planet. That is all I kept thinking.

The only bight spot to all of this was that in June of 2020 I drove across America, to Philadelphia to be there the that day Walter Ogrod got out of jail.

Laura and I drove (she covered all of Iowa and most of Oregon thankfully) 6.000 miles round trip with the girls in the back of the pickup truck bed hidden in blankets with our dog Mango.

My father loved Laura and the girls as well upon meeting them at his house, it was an easy trip for them all to meet and bond. I kept just being so humble to have this be something good for Poppy now that he had been on his own ten years since my mother died. His frail walk and aching steps made me just appreciate his mind being diverted by these English children under his charming spell. Oh Poppy was theirs now, and he had a joy I never really got to offer him with Lara Rebecca. Hey, take the win Nicky, just enjoy.

Then Mango pissed in his bed.

Mango so young and she stupidly got excited ran up into my father's bedroom, jumped on his bed, squatted down and pissed. Sharpei, Yellow Lab, mix breed dog equals big puddle of piss.

My dad found out when he went to go to bed after one of the sweetest "goodnight Poppy" kiss festivals one can imagine Bethany and Zara giving my father, just before he went and laid down in dog urine.

I should have known this was a foreboding sign, flashing red signal to be on point...my hands clench as I write this next part, I should have seen somehow all of this was Philly, pay attention.

What a shit storm that unfolded going on through out this day. Walter has one family member. His brother. Greg. What a joke of a man this guy is.

First Greg made sure to be the only one at the prison when Walter got out, sending everyone to his house that he was living in with a woman whom he was abusing. He showed up with no shoes on his feet at the prison to get Walter out of jail. It's on video... Oh and he was high as fuck on cocaine. I declined his offer of some for me to snort.

His girlfriend would tell me in her kitchen only an hour after meeting her, how this guy beat her up just the night before saying she was fired for being part of his operation. She lifted her shirt to show Laura and I her back that was full of bruises from his fists and we could not believe this shit. Oh yeah, he kept referring to himself as "The Hashman"...This made my first day home look like a fucking joke to be even complaining about!

I could not believe Walter had to be sucked dry by this duplicitous creature. There were two men on Death Row who tried to murder Greg (They killed his girlfriend, Greg survived) and it was only because of that incident that Walter got called into a police station. Only because of the near murder of Greg Walter had his life ruined when the cops got him to confess to a child's murder that just happened to have taken place on this same damn street he lived on years before.

Do you get what I was being hit with? Well it gets worse, because all of Greg's former associates start telling me all sorts of really horrible shit about Walter's brother. I filmed it all. I was in stunned disbelief as Greg would jump between talking to others and shouting at his girlfriend to not let me get into Walter's head.

Greg was so paranoid when Walter was at the house with me and I was any where near Walter and alone that at one point I had to call Walter's lawyers and tell them what was going on.

Walter's lawyers beg me on the phone to stay and offer some sort of stability to him. I told them I had to go get a hotel as my father asked us to not bring my dog back to his house again, and I could not do anything for Walter. I was so close to losing my cool witnessing his girlfriend flinch serving food, asking Laura to do it for her as she cried in the bedroom. He was so high on drugs and drinking that Greg actually hit on my wife in a scummy way while I was right coming down the basement steps. Nah, fuck this madness, we are all out of there I told Laura.

I got some contact details off of a couple guys there who set me straight about Greg and whom said they would help Walter, and I left. I explained to Walter's lawyers how I could not get involved and I could not help my friend as I had planned to do with the help of Jason Flom who had given me initial funds for Walter to come to Oregon with my family and I.

I could not make a documentary about Walter, the friendship that we had in prison and how I spent 20 years of my life fighting for this man to be set free. I could not do anything for him or myself and I was not going to jail for beating his druggie brother down in

Philadelphia.

I took the children and Laura to the ocean over in New Jersey and I let them all have some fun while I went through all kinds of lament for what I was witnessing.

Greg went to jail for violating his parole for beating on his girlfriend right after this, and Walter ended up living with total strangers to start his life of freedom.

You literally could not make this sort of shit up.

Walter rang me up once a couple months later and said that I took money that was intended for him. (true, I accepted 3.500 dollars) from Jason Flom for me to get Walter a place in Oregon so I could care for him.

I tried to explain to Walter that I could not break through the shit Greg did in front of me, and how I was

living in the woods myself, or that I spent the money on my wife and children for food, he hung up on me, and that is the lastI heard from my friend.

When I got back to Oregon my dreams of making any thing about Walter were dead. I told my friend Arthor Landon who was funding the documentary about the incredible efforts I made to free my two friends Walter Orgrod and Ernie Simmons how the project had to change.

Eventually, with the enormous help of both Mark Koops and director Lior Gellor we came up with project to replace my efforts to free others with "Life After Death"... a

documentary about post-prison life in general for four distinct human stories...

MEANWHILE A WHOLE NEW LINGERING THING...

My first scenes in this new project would be of me just getting out of jail in 2021 and screaming in frustrated anger at what just had been done to me for some shit that had happened back in 2019 and 2020, just before the pandemic hit...

Please excuse why I shortly deviate here to explain how a weird facet of my life is some folks who have money who come alone are not Arthur. This really happened this way. A woman deeply disturbed, with hidden motives right out of a horro story played with us by using her money. Things like send us to Hollywood with the Honeymoon Suite of a hotel in San Francisco paid for by her, all so I could do the DR. Phil show about me getting Walter his life back. She bought a truck for us to use, then got my gaurd down, got me to let her perform oral on me, only to then secretly collect the semen and tried to get me done. First falsely accusing me for sexual assault, then claimed I stole from her whe she was not taken as credible.

It's all true. I got charged for letting this deranged woman come in and do all manner of things. She has joined forces with Karen and has alleged I am a serial millionaire who has had the assistance of Laura in the disappearance of four people. And while the part of how I interfered with her marriage to Harry Styles from the boy band "One Direction" may be funny to hear her rant about, the first part nearly got me assaulted in England. Not even making it up, people read the shit this lunatic posts about me being a serial killer, (while they actually tell me in their deranged mind how Interpol called them) and they are sure it is all true. This Uncle Fester look alike from the Adams family who is literally riding around on a red mobility scooter shouted all this at me as I was just finishing this book here in Reading England.

That is the second most insane thing I ever thought I would have to write, that here in December 2023 I have a mobility scooter riding hater who is bent of running me down because he read I am a serial killer, who also has two multi million pound businesses, so I better watch out, because Ol' Uncle Fester is on the case!

Does it matter that the Appeals court of Oregon reversed this lie on appeal? NO, I am sure my attackers with miss that point.

That is how fucked my life is....

Now back to the story and where I was getting to my hopes that this chapter finally finds me some sort of cohesive an ending. But yeah, That's all I can come up with really... The pandemic made everyone crazy in some ways.

I have a depleted immune system from what was done to me in prison, I could not be vaccinated. I was in the group they said was more likely to die from it than get protection.

I felt like we were there in the National forest in the very beginning pandemic all the way up to 2021 so that we would not be part of this illness.

All we could do to weather out this terrible storm waiting to drop down on me outside of the forest did not matter. I did what I could, I let things go on while we lived in the woods having Christmas under the stars by a campfire.

But nothing passed really, as Laura kept us barely going with her cleaning jobs in houses and even moreover, she had a second job at a farmers market in town. We were way below enough to get housing though. If not for Laura we would have not made it. I know. I felt her struggling to keep our children there, the winter in Oregon mountains can be really brutal.

I spent the days teaching the children online being the camp cook and keeping our camp safe when the others went to town. I just kept my head down for the shame I caused Laura with that woman.

Then I severely broke my right ankle that winter, so I basically stayed in camp, hobbling on one leg. I was mostly miserable feeling like maybe that was the shit that you get in life for being all full of yourself.

I was feeling a like there was a real energy change to it all, like not just how the world lost some gleam to it from the pandemic, like no personally, more. More bad.

I felt so badly for this man Aurthor whom I had never met in life. It was only because of him and this investment to do something to try and fix my life that I hung on.

This is how it goes…Arthur learned about me from my doing the Spencer Lodge podcast in Dubai via video feed back across the globe to the garage in my house in Oregon in October 2019.

So now I had a project that was ruined, and even thanks to both Mr. Mark Koops and Lior Gellor, (And Always my angel Anthony Samadani) they all got together and tried to make this documentary to help rectify my life…just as it is being blown apart beyond anything they could do. They are all doing this whole thing for no money for themselves, Arthur was just hoping to get his investment back. When shit is lined up against you, that is just how it will be.

It gets worse by far when we go from my getting Walter out of prison just because I did the good thing, the right thing...to letting it morph to something not broken by me or by my twisted life... No, I can't tell a story with my now being the flawed hero who fucks up as badly as I did then.

Before I could even tell Aurthor how I was going to see that he did not waste his investment, just like that...Laura left the camp and she took the children, three dogs and left me with a pregnant Mango and our cat Marmite.

Yeah, don't. Just don't do any of poor Nick, fuck that I did my shit to mess this all up. I am glad God got them out of there even if it meant someone would hold Laura.

Anyone that has a woman and her children living in a shitty 2004 RV with no hope of any stability is delusional if they think someone will stay with you once you break thier heart with a stupid daliance of 15 minutes.

I deserved the slap both physical and metaphorically I share here. I buried my wedding band on the pad in Snaketooth ridge, and the others allleft camp, so it was like it was peeled apart in two swift days.

Just like that, the girls and Laura had a nice home and safety, in town, while I wondered the woods listening for a sign they would drive up to see me...

I hated how all the noise of the world coming back out of lock down was making what I was going though easy to be a nothing on everyone's radar.

So that is where I ended up in that point of wondering should I go to Los Angeles and see Anthony about the project or any way I could get speaking or work just two days later, when I got arrested.

I was at a food bank with Mango in the pick up truck, my motorhome was parked at a rest stop with Marmite locked inside. I was charged with theft but they set my bail at 70.000 US dollars, making sure I had to stay in jail with COVD. I had to get one of the men we once camped with to take Mango and the truck. I went into all this horrible shit in a ratty old jail cell while everyone whom in life I knew declined to bail me out.

I know it is a story to some, but as the camera man met me 26 days later in the early morning hours of an April morning in 2021, a fellow prisoner being set free with me shared the shit feelings of ghosts inside that former mortuary where they burned or executed humans.

The whole time I was in that cell, I had more of these crazy things hitting me and by now, so what? it is down to what will happen, just happens and figure it out.

Nasty long month in jail, being forced to plead guilty to get out (because all I faced was a probation sentence anyway, and everyone in jail was getting COVD and dying.) They held me on thier stupidly high bail to force my hand, got their plea and, not one person would help me because how could I possibly be falsely accused twice in life?

Sigh... so yes, I took their shitty deal, I was sentenced to two years probation, and I got out of jail with a film crew waiting for me out front of the Curry County jail all for me to tell the shit they just pulled on me for a woman who just played them all for fools.

When I got released I had to stay in the woods and serve out this joke of probation while I waited for Mango to give birth... Marmite got rescued and ended up with Laura and the girls.

Then of all the idiot things someone could do, one of Laura's friends tells her a tiny bit of Methamphetamine is like ADHD meds and that she will get over being all down from our break up. Just one dose of the new age version of this drug they claim can ruin your life.

It did, and I was not the one taking it...

What a horror to watch this hideous drug erase her personality and drive her mad with paranoid realities. I am not going into this, just terrible what happened.

Mango had ten puppies in the RV and I kept the first male born pup and I named him Blu. I got a job at a breakfast cafe along the Oregon coast and it was there along the Pacific Ocean I began searching for how to deal with losing the love of my life... I tried to deal with Laura, I was still trying to spend time with the girls in the RV when she brought them for me to see.

I hated knowing this drug was destroying any semblances of hope. I knew from being hooked on it years ago how hopeless that I was, to how you end up creating an alternative reality, do stupid things and ruin all.

Summer of 2021 was yet another year Beth broke an arm, I swear we were not bad parents, I bought her a penny board, she got on it rode about ten yards and flopped over and her arm was broken again!

So that has to be where I can now leave the second to hardest chapter of this book for me to write. This next and final bit is the worst, but so be it. I had the ability to live it, now I have the courage, wit, and wisdom to share it with all style I believe.

Especially after I had my laptop crash and die some 38.000 words into this work, and I had to go back and fix this whole book on a new laptop while now living in the back of my camper as it sits parked in Borehamwood England December 2023, all thanks to friends here who love me.

Even now as I read this work, I continue in wonder about why I am not batshit crazy.

Just from encounters with lunatics and deranged people who have taken this internet way too seriously.

I am so grateful that I do not watch television daily to have my brain poisoned with whom to trust.

Thankfully, I honestly think now that my incarceration itself has kept me balanced mentally with knowing what the mainstream will believe is so far from reality. I know to how stay in my lane and not get caught up in it all.

I am focused on how to deal with my challenges, the way forward, and how to process my own grief.

How dare I ignore all of that to be politically outwardly driven, or opinionated over anyone else?

When you live through terrible things like I have, you have enough self respect to never lose sight of it all.

I am not saying that I have some magic gift to process grief better than any one else, I just tried to find some meaning to it all that does not make me fall to pieces, or think that I have to take on some cause to override my empty and pathetic life.

Anyway, despite whatever rumors will always be spread about me now or when I die, I am so glad that I am now able to set all of this record right in this written work.

I am so grateful that there are a number of people who can verify every single portion of this book.

That is how we leave this chapter, so I can just now go and do this last part justice...

CHAPTER SIX: FLIP THIS ONE REAL GOOD, AND WOW...

In September of 2021 I met Alex Rotoli while I was camping in Pistol River Oregon. The craziest series of events unfolded. I met a woman named Crystal inside of a shop in Gold Beach Oregon. She told me what a delight it was that I was so polite as she served me. She told me a story of a patron at her other job serving food who had spit in her face for not wearing a mask while serving food to the woman who actually had spit on her.

She then told me to come to her other place of work because they needed a morning cook. I got hired on the spot when I met the owner John. I soon took Mango and Blu in my little Geo Tracker car that I was towing behind the RV, back and forth to work from my RV parked back at Pistol River beach.

On my second day of my bringing home food that I was allowed to make for myself at work, (saving it to have for my dinner each night when I finished), I met a man who had parked right next to my RV. It was that night that was the Philly Cheessteak sandwhiches of all things which I made that really made us connect. His favorite food.

You see, Alex was just then getting out of his car when I pulled up just at that very moment. His dog named Bishop is a mixed breed boxer that was with him, and soon as Blu saw him, they tore off together towards the sand on the beach with Alex walking to follow them.

   About 40 years old, but frail and walking with a cane, and yet he had a physique of an athlete at one point, there was no doubt that from his frame.

   Alex told me his name and that he was originally from Virginia. I told him my name and that I was from Pennsylvania. Alex said that he did not mean to crowd in on my beautiful place to park, while I assured him how I welcomed having someone to hang out with. I said how I had fresh Philly Cheesesteaks from work and he could have one with me back at camp.

   That was it for us as friends. We right away soon learned how we were both huge Philadelphia Eagles football fans, that he and I both played the position of Saftey on the defence.

   We both loved a player named Eric Allen who played the positon of Safety for the Eagles back in the early 1990's.

   Instantly I just knew something big waas afoot from how I pulled up as he was even then deciding to stay or go,... he even said how he passed my spot twice and only then pulled over to meet me like this...so yes, just somehow I knew this was not by chance or happenstance my meeting this human.

   I was dealing with a lot, I was holding down a job while I did my best to not fall to bits for losing Laura and the girls. I was even able with grace to make meals for the very Judge who sentenced me to probation and his entire staff to my highest effort without being rude or disrespectful. I swear on all I hold dear that is true. I always was polite and nice to the Sheriff and his staff, I honestly knew what was done to me was all the work of a nutjob. If I did anything out of spite to anyone while I cooked food I would prove myself worthy of such lies.

So no, I got my head down, learned how to make some fantastic eggs benedict, and many amazing foods, all while feeding the stuffing out of my friend Alex. We had two amazing weeks nearly while the last of the clear days without rain played out.

I have to tell you why I so love Alex Rotoli for being able to come into my life as he did and when he did.

You see, a man like this is not on the stage, doing any big efforts because he got things done to him. No, Alex is like millions of men who get Cancer.

When I met Alex he was 9 years nearly into being told every six months he will die. Imagine, each time you go see your doctors, they are incredulous that you are back again with bone cancer so rare that less than 50 humans have ever had it. The chopped his leg to shit, they told him he had zero chance of survival. And...he did it all living in a car with his dog.

You know those "Oh Shit, tell me this is not real" kind of moments we all get hit with? That kept happening the more Alex told me how he had a woman like my Laura and she had two little girls like I once had...now he just had Bishop and friends in America who let him sofa surf and get showers.

I loved this man's determined natured to find meaning. I swaer, I could not wait each day to come back from work when the cafe closed around 2:pm so that I could bring food home that Alex and I ate as we talked and talked into the night about our lives. I let my man go on for a least a whole week of telling me all the many trials and tributes of his medical journey before I even told him about my life, or about the way I had ended up there.

I let this man have the decency and the dignity to tell me in full who he was so that when I shared my won story he said that he was relieved that he finally found someone who did not either feel overwhelmed by his ordeal, or crudely ask him why he did not just kill himself and not suffer so badly in this way.

You do know that is real? People, disgusting people asked my friend why he did not just kill himself. When Alex related that to me, and how he felt for having someone say that to him, I swore if I could,... I was going to give this man the best effort any friend could to tell the world his beautiful story. It was like I am the one person whom Alex could have met who would be willing to inspire him to live and hang on, as I then set about a way to tell his fantastic view of it all on film.

Just so that we are clear, and by the time this book is read by many, I got gifted with how to now tell my freind Alex Rotoli's story because of an optical brilliance of having the Milkyway, with its many stars light up the calm ocean before us. I was standing by the camper one night, when I turned and I shouted for Alex to look, please look at this amazing sight...

No street lights for miles, no houses out on that coast to distort the pitch black night in Oregon. Aside from the logging trucks or a few cars passing by, it is deep dark skies all above.

Alex and I stood while being transfixed by seeing this huge ribbon of stars that is the Milky Way both in the sky, and it's reflection that was on the calmest sea possible. There before us the ocean's surface glittered with billions of stars illuminating it all! I never saw anything like that in my life. We were so overcome with joy, we were shouting about what we each saw. Alex was so excited he said that this was just like when he went to Scotland once, and how he could not understand this weird feeling of being so alive...even while having cancer!

   I looked at this man. All around me nothing mattered as I stood looking at the emotion of what it felt for him to feel alive for just a tiny amount of time. It was the most beautiful thing I could have seen that night. I knew right then what I was going to do, and what the title of this film was going to be. I mean it screams itself out does it not? "Why Don't You Just Kill Yourself"? That's it.

   When you are stuck living a shit life and you share your traumas with others, only for them to be crass enough to ask why don't you end your life, you give them the Alex Rotoli badass reply to their stupidity with who you become. My friend dreams of writing a book called "The Human Owner's Manual", you know like for an automobile, with a list of contents and ideas for operating your body. Alex loves life enough to be decent.

   I swore to this man, I told him forcefully to his face that I would come see him in Washington state where he was registered for medical treatments in a few months of when we met. I told him I would be there in the spring of 2022 so that we could celebrate his next 6 months of defying the odds, and if he did not make it, I would come and get Bishop. I said no matter what I was going to now chase money to get his documentary to be brought to life. The only sad part to the whole thing was Mango bit Bishop for being so close to her baby Blu. Once again Mango fucked shit up.

The six months came, but so much changed from the beach and my staying there in winter. I found what I thought was the perfect job for me after Alex left though.

I read an ad on Facebook that offered housing and a salary to care for horses on a ranch that had handicapped
children on it. My duties would be to care for the horses and the property, and that my dogs were welcome as well.

Okay, I had zero equestrian training, never ran a ranch or did farm work, and aside from how I once got kicked seriously by a horse, I was not at all qualified to do the job. I bluffed my way though the interview playing as home down as I could in front of the owners. I wanted to try to stay in this one spot so that I could leave the RV there and go see Alex in Washington, especially since he was not sure how his next bone scans were going to come out.

Working with horses was so much a great thing for me
mentally. I had a pony named Peaches fall in love with Blu and each morning that I fed her Blu got kisses from his hottie with all that blonde hair. I had 70 acres of land to tend to, a cow named Curly, 3 assorted types of horses and it was all next to a lake in the Mountains.

What a blessing to have this job, be away from all my hardships as I got to help children who would thrash in a chair all day, only to then sit quietly when I brought Peaches around so that they spent time with the animal in comfort.

Watching that kind of event on a near daily basis made all kinds of healing happen for me. I honestly loved my working there, and they were nice to me in their understanding how I had lost my wife and children.

Alex did not need me to go see him where he lived in six months from our first camping together, he came down to the ranch in Oregon and camped at the front of the property I worked on. Alex camped in his car with his dog Bishop (Well away from Mango!) and he did so in order for us both to set up a fire pit up there for us to watch TV and eat.

We used the Television set out there to watch the NFL spring draft of college players coming into the league that year.

How cool that as we both loved the Philadelphia Eagles, this was pure joy for us to have a big TV set up on a table, a beautiful lake in the back drop, and we are sharing the best sports event one could have together.

For three days Alex and I spent some of the very best moments two friends could share during this trip he made there in spring of 2022. I made food for us like I used to do when I worked in the restaurant back in Pistol River. I amazed my friend over and over telling him who would be drafted and why. Again and again I chose right, and he loved my knowledge and passion for this sport. I was so proud of that. That was some of the best parts of a year of joy that I had working that job. For me to that point, when my friend Alex came and spent time with me I was so happy to show him how I was doing well mentally after all the shit with Walter and Laura.

We both said that when he parted that time, how we would make sure I would come to Washington and see him after his next health in six months. That "next time" felt so assured then, and we were so close as pals too, we really did think things would be okay.

No way did I know that parting of ours on the ranch was the last time that I would have full use of my left eye again in life, or how I would be put on a whole new level of medical challenges in my life.

It's just that quick how it can all go awry.

The weekend that Alex left I went back to resurfacing the driveway as part of my duties.

I had just finished laying down concrete repairs on the driveway of the ranch where I worked to where it was nearly done. I was so proud of how strong that I was from all the hard work I did that year.

I Felt for the first time in years like I was really healing all the damage from different falls or whatever…Just really fit from long days on a ranch.

So, there I was feeling all good about me, and I went into town with both dogs in the Geo Tracker auto that I used.

It was in bright sunlight that was soon to be nightfall as it always is in the winter when I left. As I drove down the mountain road that I lived on, I entered a turn at the bottom that had not gotten any sunlight that day. Still frozen over with a thin sheet of "black ice" as it is called, I had no chance to do anything when I lost control going around the corner of this icy road.

I spun my car completely around, hit the side of the road, flipped over twice as both dogs went flying through the front window of the car.

Oh how my heart sank as I called Mango to me as she whimpered on the roadside. That is my first memory after the car stopped after the crash sounds. I was just standing by the car calling Mango. Blu was no where to be seen andat first I thought he was trapped under the upside down car,so I tried to lift it with my bare hands.

I got smashed good in this wreck.

Not many broken bones, a finger on the gear shift hand, and something popped in my lower back, but my head was not right for sure.

135

Two hours after flipping the car I managed to get Blu to come back from the woods with help from others. I still to this day do not remember getting my seat belt undone, nor climbing out of the car to stand there and call Mango.

I would wake up the next morning and have a floating thing in my left eye. I don't know how, but I just handled all of this without freaking out that night somehow. I called my friend Jason who lives down down in Los Angeles late that night as I lay in bed with my two injured dogs...he asked me why I was not all freaked out to be so close to death again.

I said that the first time when I got stabbed in prison, I panicked. The 5th time that I got stabbed in prison, I knew to actually stay calm to stop the blood loss. I said to him that in honestly, it's just like that kind of example now.

I went to a Hospital in Del Norte California and began to have brain scans taken because I now have cognitive issues after the car crash. With already having a history of childhood brain injury from when I was raped and a beaten in the head with a field stone by a local man in my neighborhood, this now has made my situation very hard.

CTE brain injury syndrome, a degenerative condition commonly associated with a sports injury. That is what I now have to deal with.

With eye impairment and a history of concussions before and while inside prison, this car wreck scrambled my head a bit.

By the 6th scan of my brain in later 2022 I was told I have a plaque build up on my skull that is common with this illness, and that I was in unchartered waters, as each individual beset by this injury is different.

Some kill themselves while being driven mad by the bleakness it causes. Others murder humans in singular or in mass killings. There is no way to gauge what would unfold going forward with me, but that this last head injury was going to have to be the the very last. Any more blows to the head and I risked stroke, death or paralysis from this more head trauma.

You cannot image how broken I felt both from being so
weary of being homeless in the mountains, as well as now being told why I have this cloud in my head. I could not afford top of the line health care, I could not help things to be better while living in isolation in the woods. Because that is where I ended up next.

Not long after the car wreck the owners decided to move off the land as they had to sell it. I couldn't believe that I was left injured again, and now I had to go find a new job and a place to park. I had to find a place for the dogs and I to live without conflict.

Just like that, it all seemed to go towards this end with me now having constant headaches all the time.

I managed to move onto a piece of land not far from the
ranch that was land that was also right next to a huge marijuana farm that was run by two Bulgarian brothers.

I had befriended them over time, as they had a shared driveway to their land behind the ranch, so I saw them daily for months during the growing season.

When they heard the place was up for sale and I was out of work they told me how they wanted me to move back there for my dogs to ward off thieves, so they said I could stay for free back there.

I got another job at a pizza based restaurant in the area,
and I built a large enclosure in the woods next to my RV for the dogs to be kept inside of while I worked in town nearby.

Surely I had to figure this out somehow. It all seemed to be such a dark time for me, not just all the days I spent alone lamenting my loss in my RV, but my mind was not as it was before then.

All I could do is try to bring to life the failed project about getting Walter out of jail, we began the project titled "Life After

Death", which is now a series of post release stories of men and women who were wrongfully convicted.

My part in this would be an extraordinary effort that. I had to drive across America, back to my father's house one last time and be filmed going to my mother's grave site (my first time since her death), and go then be filmed in a prison where I was stabbed in the chest by another inmate, and then go on the very spot where I was raped and beaten senseless as a child.

How grueling an ordeal, for me to drive 300 miles to go and tell the camera in each setting whatever I was asked then and there. Pull this off mentally and maybe let everything that happened these past four years go I said in January of 2023 as I set off from Oregon.

The drive alone nearly killed me. I went from a river of rain over head to sub zero conditions at times, on into a tornado, and then another out right blizzard all made 6.000 plus miles of driving round trip a once in

a lifetime journey itself. It was like nothing was going to compare to this madness.

Starting off in a 2001 Chrysler PT Cruiser with a tow box of supplies and camping gear on the back thanks to a cago hitch I mounted, I began a drive in January of 2023 which would end in a manner that made me realize that my life in America had to finally end once and for all.

As I drove down into California from Oregon, I nearly hit an Elk in a down pouring rain storm within the first four hours. I barely managed to hold on and avoided going over a cliff along the coast. Just like that, within hours of leaving I had a near catastrophic accident.

That made me stop and consider pulling up some place and let the weather clear. Managing to get just south of that "Atmospheric River of water" they are called in Northern California, I rested in the Mojave desert for a few days.

One of the best camping I ever did with my two dogs. I was in heaven as I got to watch TV that I brought powered by two deepp cycle batteries I installed in the car with a power converter.

I camped in paradise with Coyotes and prong horned sheep passing our campsite.

When the biggest storm passed over head I got all our stuff packed and I left there only to drive into a huge freak snow storm that came from the south of the state of New Mexico. Things just kept being like this all across the USA during the drive.

Thousands of miles later I hit an area where a Tornado passed over me in the state of Tennessee that was just dropping tress all over the roads as I crept through the after math.

Finally ahead of it all entering the last few hundred miles of driving as that huge storm followed me, I drove through the last two days of rain to reach Pennsylvania.

I tried to ask my father if the two dogs and I could stay in his basement for a couple days when I finally got there, but since Mango pissed on his bed the last time I showed up, he said no to my being there.

I was hurt, but I get it…he was nearly 90 years old and it was too much with two huge dogs being around.

The film team whom I was there in town to meet from Mark Koops office got me a room at a hotel nearby, and I got myself together as best that I could mentally to do the effort for this documentary.

Walking around Philly for what I feel still so surely was my last time I will ever go there, I thought about so many things that happened in life. No way I would have ever imagined I would come back and finish like I was concluding my life. Like this is all that is left of Nicky Yarris. That kid who grew up on Milan street.

Being there to go to places that held all of my darkest moments was daunting. I had to get through this, this had to be some of my healing, not my ultimate ruination.

I needed some good to come out of this for me to take all of it forward. That was my whole mantra over and over.

When the film team came to meet me I was shocked that Mark Koops came personally. In all the many years that this man has worked, he was never in front of the lens as he was about to be here. If not for Mark and his patience with Lior the whole thing nearly fell apart at my father's house.

I knocked on his door, only I got it wrong thinking Poppy would not answer. He was so frail he did not hear me there. Mark and Lior got him to answer when I walked off if disheartened disappointment, thinking it was all shit. They called me back to his door and as timidly as I could I wnet into Poppy's house and I did the interview with him. I got a hug at the end of iit, but it felt so horrible to be in the midst of this.

Lior came with me down to the basement and I tried to tell him about mmy first night out of prison down there. This was the most difficult effort I ever did. I nearly wanted to burst with sadness. I looked at my dad and I saw what the 12 years he lived without my mother to care for him had done. The weary pains were obvious on him as he spoke to the camera, piously saying he had no kind of life and all he had was suffering.

Mike Yarris worked himself to a state of being bent over in sorrow and he was barely able to walk a few steps with help of a walker.

By then My father had to pee in a pot on a stool that my family got for him to use as a portable toilet, but he was not wanting any of this.

At the end, after we did a most awkward interview before the cameras, I leaned in and hugged my father for what was my last time in life. I just knew it. He was so frail in my arms, he really was not doing well.

I felt like it was so much like all the many times that I spent the last days of others lives in prison, there is this web of feelings we are witnessing of this thing...it is one where someone has the last of life within sight. They almost make you able to see where they are looking off towards. I don't like that feeling.

You don't project sorrow then, it's more of a want to comfort and express a bond that they are carrying with you to their end is what I did. Poppy was going to join my mother soon, I was glad I was just getting to see him this onelast time, so it was right that I had already made up my mind to leave the United States.

I told my father my plans. That I had been back in touch with Laura back in the UK, and with her having a new job and being sober, how we were going to reunite for the sake of her two girls seeing us happy. I told my father how I needed help with my brain injury as well as how the UK allowed me free health care for my condition.

No matter what we had been through, I needed his validation to go and try and help heal what happened between Laura and I. I did not want to be Poppy without my Jayne.

Next after my filing with my father, I went and let myself be filmed visiting my mother's grave. It was just near her Birthday and I was not handling this well.

I was at this point really of just putting on bravery for everyone, I really was not doing well with thinking about what was to lie ahead for me after I got done at my mother's resting spot. I did as best that I could to be filmed over and over, with my mother's grave being the central point to retakes I did not dwell on how I was nearly crumbling inside each time I did another take, another angel, then a drone shot, and one more take from you over here... Wow, just wow.

Going to the old main prison in Philadelphia and being

filmed on the very spot where I got stabbed in the chest and sharing all manner of that type of previous life that I once knew felt like a break in the endurance level efforts I went through.

I had that omnipresent feeling of knowing that the big finish was me taking a film team back to the very spot where I got raped as a child.

I got through it. Okay? I made out better than I thought I would, but it hurt. I held on tight mentally, got my shit together enough to perform, and I got through three things that hurt me very deeply.

I want so much to get past all of this to share what happened after I left Philadelphia, yet its so important for all to know what led to this last bit while I was reeling from being filmed doing the worst retelling of my childhood.

I left Philadelphia with my two dogs feeling like that was my last bit of blood or tears that I had to shed in a lifelong battle to pay for who I was in life. I don't care what anyone says, in view of all the sheer heartbreaking and degrading manner of life that I was forced to live, just all in this one book, I hold aloft that I really have not done much to deserve so much of it all.

I keep right on paying all of my dues without my snapping out mentally and harming others, I keep trying to find meaning no matter what I do, or I have done to me. I am not adding another chapter to this book after this one. It has just come to me now, this thought of how I must finish it all Nicky, just tell these last bits and no need for a big long flourish to anything, just let go please.

This is me now sharing with you all how it played out for me from this point of leaving Philly in 2023 to these last pages written here in December of 2023.

I have to somehow now mentally end my own hurts as I write this last part out. This book is my cathartic efforts to heal (and leave a linear written effort) so that anyone who cares about me finds out all that happened. That's it really. My daughter Lara will read this. She will see what to judge or love me for after she reads this.

So are you Ready? I am. I swear now how I am so ready to stop and lift my head up from all this broken life, and after I complete this written work, I walk away from so much more than just America. I walk away from this being picked on crap, and stalker assholes with nutjobs who read lies about me online and attacking me when they don't know shit. This is my life of freedom and this is my story of living here with the most amazing life.

I am telling my side of my own life so that not one single person who has ever tried to hurt me sees how they had accomplished anything more than inspiring me.

I completed my drive back to Oregon from Philadelphia, but I got stuck in another Blizzard in Colorado, ended up watching the whole world turn frigid and brutal all the way back. I was only there briefly wondering what I was going to do to live now that I finished my work with the documentary, when I got invited to Los Angeles to film an episode of Soft White Underbelly Podcast.

Another 1500 miles of driving this would take.

I also had my beloved dog Mango die in my arms in a tragic accident in Los Angeles.

Unbelievable as it seems right on the very beach where Anthony Samadani had married Laura and I back in 2017. I had been camping at Playa Del Vista Beach and this is where it happened.

This was so fucked up, so surreal, I knew it was sealing my determination to get away from all this sorrow before I took my own life.

Did you know in 2023 a rare Blizzard hit Los Angeles while I was doing this podcast? Look it up on the news.

Yeah well, I don't care as much about it as it so seemed part of this next crazy bit...

I went into downtown Los Angeles to Skid row and I did 1 hour and 39 minutes beautifully of a Podcast
episode that had not one single question to it.

I thought so much about this all as I drove there from Oregon that I asked to do it my own way. I spoke of the perspective of being born twice.

I made the analogy of being born first in Philadelphia, and what that life was like, to then speak about being born a second time at age 42 after Death row.

My whole hope for doing this podcast was that I wanted to see if I still had the mental fluidity to do a narrative driven soliloquy about my life's journey after the car wreck fucked my head up. I wanted to see how
mentally sharp I still was. I had to go forward and promote my Cancer project for Alex, so I had to try and get back to speaking, or doing things online like this podcast. I was too injured for labor based work, if I was going to get him help this was it.

I stayed in Los Angeles waiting for the rare Blizzard that
hit the area to pass while I camped on the beach. I lost two tents, One I brought with me and one Anthony paid for when the first one got shredded by the winds.

Two days after that the podcast was aired was the morning Mango got her collar stuck in Blu's mouth and she choked to death in my arms as I screamed for help.

This triggered so much pain for how Jaymie Leigh had
died in my arms.

I was gutted when I learned that despite my efforts to shield Laura from her learning about this tragic death of our beloved dog, that Karen got a hold of this information from one of her recently recruited, and mentally vulnerable minions in her stalking efforts.

Karen made sure Laura learned about this death and crushed Laura with it.

I know, you don't have to say it, but you have to be next level sinister as a person to use this poor animal's death like this, and I will never forget this low act for all my days.

All I did was tell a Karen-subverted "follower" who was being so supportive of my journey to do my work, (someone who had found me on Instagram and befriended me there), all about the death of my dog while in tears.

Only for that person to have been already been under the guile of my stalker and sent it straight to Karen.

Karen got ahold of my message about Mango dying in my arms and literally sent it to Laura.

This was done to ruin my hopes of coming back to be with Laura. On the Podcast episode I said I was still in love, and that one line out of 1 hour and 39 minutes is what I promise you made her go mental.

I know, just like losing the baby and being tormented about a time stamp of a "Tweet", I have to have my stalker use the death of a dog whom I cherished as a weapon to fuck with my head. The police in the UK won't help me, I filed numerous reports with them only to be told how this is just some civil matter because all this is, is just someone smearing my reputation. Seriously, this is the

exactly the words I was told here in England when II tried to file charges in 2023.

You see, I had to call my friend Noah and tell him how I lost my dog, how he had to come help me please. Noah came with his girlfriend and they took Blu for me in his car. I asked him to bring me a shovel and I said goodbye to my baby boy as I took off for the desert outside of LA.

I drove for hours with my dead dog in the back of the car.

Yep, I really wanted to dig a whole in that ground big enough for me and my darling dog to climb into. If you knew me back then and you saw me with my dogs, you knew I loved them tremendously. Their loss from my life has deeply scarred me as much as any other event in life. To have had this event have been used as a battering club by Karen just felt so cheap, so cowardly.

When I was burying Mango in the ground that day as I swore that in a crazy eerie way God was speaking to me, guiding me with fierce winds as I dug into the earth. I felt somehow this was all telling me in this mass of energy how I was to not give in.

I don't care what anyone thinks of my mental state that day, I know what I heard. I knew what I had to do...

I got up off my knees after I finished my prayers for Mango's energy to please find me again in the next life, and I got in my car and I gave my tent and everything in it to the homeless back at Play Del Vista Beach. I went back to Oregon.

I was getting out of there as soon as I could and I did not care what I had to leave to behind do so.

I cut off the nasty co-conspirator Karen was working with to torment me, told Laura to ignore that jealous and mentally deranged shit, and that I was coming for her.

I gave my motorhome to a family living on the pot farm next to where I was living that also had a handicapped daughter with them. I did it so they could get away from the drugs and guns all day every day that were there.

I gave my car to my friend Chris who worked on the Pot farm in exchange to him to drive me up to Washington state for me to Fly out of the USA. I didnt care that he smoked meth as he drove and I tried to rest from this mad beat down I just lived, I was shattered to the point of I don't give a shit.

The release of the Podcast "Soft White Underbelly" got me help that I needed to get back to the UK with a very brief "GOFundME" account that Karen got attacked and taken down with help of her recruits. I got a flight back to England March 20th 2023 only to have my passport confiscated because Karen, got my passport information for her idiot minion who had previously tried to dupe me into thinking she had gotten me an airline ticket home. Then they reported my passport stolen or lost.

Luckily I have a visa allowing me to live here, so the UK government showed love, let me in and despite Karen's best efforts, I came to the UK only to have no papers, no country, and no housing.

I ended up going to see Laura at her work at a hotel straight from the airport. I wanted so much for the absolute maddening events to just get out of America could somehow now be over.

How could anyone find healing like this I wondered. I sincerely needed England to hold the key to my holding on in life.

From the obvious way there are not many pages to follow this one I find myself on here, how I am not going to drag this out while covering the rest is my battle. I just cannot keep doing this much more, this story portion needs to end.

I will just segue into it in this way…I really wanted to love Laura and what he shared was so huge in my life that I wanted her to be the one.

I told anyone who heard my Podcast appearances since I got back to the UK, and I told myself this as well.

I was living out of a car that I got on credit with a man named Nick who lived up north while I was staying inside of it in the Reading area of England.

But sadly Laura was still messing around with hard drugs. And one last time she put her hands on me as I drove my car was all I could take this time.

Seriously, after what I was put through, I don't

need that shit, and my health can not let me be around arguing and violence. I really just am not allowed to be caught up in all of that upheaval. My CTE will get so bad I cannot deal with this.

Then as I was about to feel all destroyed for it, that was shown to be the only way Laura could get help, as she nearly died from health issues just then.

In fact as I write this, the prognosis of her living is dim.

I have no right to discuss her medical condition but I am praying each day as I finish this book that they get her into surgery and save her life.

Just please just let me do this one last portion without it all overwhelming you all my gracious readers. I have to talk about one last part with Alex, okay?

The only amazing thing that came out of all of this to my point of now, while being back in the UK for all of this reunion effort with my wife is how I met a film director named Mikey Perry at Laura's job.

Mikey Perry is right now as I write this book making the documentary about Alex. He just completed days of filming with Alex in Washington here in December 2023.

Mikey and I met because of a bag of Jelly Beans that i had with me ironically.

I had a bag of jelly beans stuck under the passenger seat of my car that I was driving from my former father in laws house in Cowbit England, going down to see Laura at her work. I could not reach them the whole drive, and I was so hungry that it was like a sad joke. But for some crazy reason, I left them there until I got out of the car and I took them into the hotel and put them down with a flourish on the bar inside the hotel.

A man walks over named MIke Perry, he has a son named MIkey Perry and this mans begins telling me all about his relations to this Jelly bean company. No way, My father Mike, his son named Mikey, this man named Mike and his son also named Mikey. What does Mikey do? Film maker.

We have an instant bond, but I am so drawn to this moment, I chase Mikey down at the play area in the hotel with my last copy of my first book. I insisted that he contact me and how I knew he would make the film we would title "Why Don't You Just Kill Yourself". It was just something you had to be there and feel what happened when I met Mikey Perry to get this fully.

While Mikey went back to Australia and I put him in touch with Alex, while I did podcasts all year for money.

What I mean is, if you want me to talk and help you get paid, pay me to come there on your podcasts. I got tired of everyone wanting me to do their podcasts and I got the pleasure of sharing a story I paid for and nothing else.

So, I got my hustle on. I got anywhere from 100 pounds to thousands of pounds to talk.

I also managed to reach over 100.000 million viewers online doing my podcast efforts.

I got enough money sent to me from Jimmy Rex in Utah, whom I met on the Instagram platform for Alex and I to buy a small RV to complete our film in.

This man Jimmy Rex and his crew that is called "THE THEY" came through for Alex and I when I told Jimmy how I was over here making the film documentary about Alex's cancer journey. This makes me so honored when men whom I never met, gets me set up in a tiny RV for me to live inside of while I wait for Alex to come over.

I cannot wait until we all finish this film that is based on a promise for me to go to Scotland and "Feel Alive" with Alex one more time. That is entirely the whole premise of the film.

We met, he told me about felling alive on the beach and I swore we would both feel alive in that way one day in Scotland just as he once felt it before meeting me.

My brain injury situation is improved for having others to talk to now that I don't live in the woods, I have a few projects going with hopes that 2024 is a good year, and my dreams of having a career come about are still alive.

It won't get easier. I know that. Laura is not having it easy health wise, I am back in touch with her, we are still talking to one another. I love her and always will. She is the only one whom I ever met who has had as hard, or worse of a life as I have in so many ways.

All this year I was so looking forward to coming over

here to join me, He endured all of my ups and downs that I went through since I got here to the UK.

Alex saved his money and he purchased airline tickets to fly here in September of 2023 so that we could then go to Scotland. I was so anxious and happy to take this little RV that Jimmy gave me money to purchase, and I was so close to being able to fulfill our dream of going there to

make him happy...

Then a couple days before he was set to fly to England Alex collapsed from infection and went into a coma.

I rung his phone over and over, not hearing from him. Then a man I never met before in life answered Alex's phone for him as he stood next to his hospital bed. It was then that he told me the sad news about Alex...

Honestly, I was so broken hearted, so feeling like if only I had tried harder somehow, that I could have gotten him here sooner.

I really did think this was it for him, for me and his dream, just all of it.

Well, Alex is harder than life, because after nearly a week of being unconscious, he wakes up and not only has his mental faculties in tact despite meningitis infection, but then twenty six tumors left his body.

Yeah I know, all the haters are going to scream that I am making this up, wait for the film, eat your popcorn and shut up when you see how this really happened.

After weeks of my thinking this guy is dead, done, it is all over, a recent scan has shown that 26 cancer tumors

disappeared, and that the ones that are left have shrunken as well!

Mikey Perry and I cannot believe this man is still going,

still proving everyone wrong about his prognosis. MiKey just got all of this amazing recovery on film, Im just sharing here how that has made me realise that I am far from done doing my part.

So yeah I continue to try and raise funds to get Alex and a film team here to complete this filming of Alex and I visiting Scotland, I even put Mikey Perry in touch with Mark Koops.

Now finish this book and then I will have began my own healing efforts on my own while I wait for Alex to get here.

I am working on helping others with suicide and

depression here in the UK. I stay on the phone constantly

with Alex to keep us both connected to this dream we each have to do something with his life's story to help millions of others to find hope.

I recently went to my own search of feeling alive as Alex did by visiting my ancestral homeland of Ireland. As soon as I got there I began to feel what Alex tried to express to me long ago...

Ireland kissed me so hard that she stole my breath away with its beauty and magnificence.

Going there and being embraced so sensuously just shook me awake and made me smile anew.

There are moments in life so remarkable that they sear

into your soul, and this was what Alex had meant for me to know I now see.

I fell into a realm internally of seeing how I could live now as no other time in my past from that one encounter of going to Dublin.

Being there I felt as if I could now live the same way as a fabled character like the "Count Of Monte Cristo" from a Dumas novel that was written long ago.

I could be mentally back in Rome when I first got out, when I was still so tender of heart, back to that time

with me sharing a cup of coffee with a beautiful woman, all for the sake of knowing the true difference between being alive, vs just living life day to day.

Long before I met Alex I understood that want which so many of us have, a wanting or to crave that special feeling of "alive".

Mine was born from the many days I suffered unjust things, Alex's was born of a medical condition no one should have to endure the likes of which.

All I have to do now is mind my own heart so that I don't

break it so badly that I want to quit.

I already have a brain condition that makes it hard for me to endure things on a daily basis, why add to it with negative actions and thoughts?

I thought back when I first got out of prison that I was a

humble man, willing to take on a promise to my mother to be kind and polite. Now I know that I am a humbled man in life, far beyond what I first felt, full stop.

I still walk around with this same wonder of why it is that my dreams keep unfolding, or that I had such dreams long before I got out, or how I keep ending up exactly where I am meant to be with perfectly time meetings or events with others. Either way this is my destiny unfolding.

In January of 2024 I will have reached 20 years of freedom.

I told myself when I forst got out that if I pulled of a miracle and made it another 23 years, that I would have taken back the same amount of years that the state took from me. Then I saw that the days since my release were as hard as any that I had encountered while on Death Row, so I soon saw the folly of my initial thoughts.

I now accepted the bigger truth that all of my life has been this one long journey of me finding those answers which only I can find from it all.

I believe so much more now than I ever did in the past. Instead of not wanting to believe anything, I am at times an easy victim for me to be swept up in others promises. I don't wanna change.

And yes, I get taken for a ride at times, or I get played for a sucker by lame folks, But I am shown why I was meant not to have that person in my life. I always get clear of their shallowness

My stalker will never stop being driven by a warped pathology. I am embarrassed for my daughter who has to witness all of this.

All I can do is throw up my hands and apologetically offer this entire story was written here as to my own folly as well as anyone else being an idiot to me.

I hold some responsibility no matter how small, so I am willing to say up front I am not a victim totally. But damn it all, this now exposes the crowd stalking which I have had aimed at me for years.

Ireland so far has been my last night of which I have had this terrible reoccurring nightmare that has haunted me for 7 years.

Its always the same...I find the baby dead in her crib, I cannot stop the events as they happened where I run to her but unlike in life, I cannot lift Jaymie, my arms are numb as I scream for someone to help pick her up.

That has been so fucked up on me to handle, and I swear I do not know why I am not insane from all of this horrible shit I deal with.

But I also swear than ever since I left Jaymie Leigh's ashes at the Trinity Colleges in Dublin this year, how I have not been getting tormented in my sleep.

Somehow I knew I had to go to Dublin, how I finally had to let go of walking around with a dead child's ashes tucked into my wallet, I finally stopped feeling broken for all the ways I drove my self crazy to be in love in life.

Now I am learning to understand what it means to mind my heart. Love is intrinsic, and love means so much to us that it is the one reason why we shed so many terrible yesterdays, just for one brilliant day of love tomorrow.

I know who I am. I know that if I keep blocking out the noise of the few, and I cling to this dream that I gave myself when I first got released from prison, then I can find the days of joy that I worked for one day.

Poverty has been my greatest blessing. I have made more deeply moving connections in life because I was homeless as I am right now, than any which I could have made from being in a mansion.

All of the many times when I was dismissed by others, hurt, and the times I got used by the wealthy, they could never tarnish the many connections which I made on the streets. That is my victory.

Wherever you are while reading this book, I want you to know how much I really appreciate your taking time to read this journaling of my life with you being privy to how I think about it all now. I promise you I am still willing to meet "you", the ones who are like me in kindness. I am so glad that I made it this far along, that I was able to show everyone that despite everything I have shared, my belief in Neuroplasticity is real and it works.

I should be so mentally destroyed, so unable to function and yet here I am, each day spent helping the next person heal. Instead of teetering on mental collapse, I am making others see a way through their own troubles.

That is the Nick Yarris affect. I just really am that way for being sent of one of life's most complex sojourns.

This surely is demonstrative proof that what I began with as a simple promise to my mother, has now become a life long offsetting ability for me to be mentally strong in the face of crushing events.

My mother had a saying she shared. She told me that there billions of "People" on earth, but that there were only so many "Human Beings". What she meant was that these are the ones who do all the good in life for others…

My mother told be to go be one of them.

I am okay with how I truncated this story, here now, I don't need thousand and thousands of more words. This is enough for anyone to share about their

freedom frankly.

Now I want to go write fiction, create stories and try to

entertain others. I even began a comedy career effort while I was in Dublin because I am just so tired of others crying from learning my story.

I needed to write this book because I am hoping that with a new book, like so many times before now, I can get enough money and move forward in motion, go on to get my own place to live maybe while sharing my speaking.

This is me, wanting so much for this to be the upswing and good I been praying for.

I find myself half way smiling for my being the come back kid of all time for pulling off a huge example of my talent and writing this book despite brain injury.

That needs to be where this all stops in this writing.

I just am trying to get going, to pick myself up one more time while Alex does his part. I know only to be the man that I began this journey as being back in 2004...

I started life a second time abck then, and then I found of who I am as an adult for having doing so ever since.

I like who I am, I love what I can be to others. I hold no grudges, everyone is going to get dirt tossed on them at some point, so I focus of healing with a brain that has a few scratched up parts inside of it.

I don't plan on doing this again. I just felt like okay...I

don't know a whole lot of people who have had a life so wild that they had to write three separate books to tell it.

Let anything after this be written in epitaph from an some other's hand, one whom I had profoundly touched hopefully.

My daughter Lara knows who I am personally by the way. I will try my best to connect with her in some way without it being a challenge of loyalties between her mother and I. That's just more of another person being petty that she does not deserve from me.

If you read this book and meet my child, please share really good things with her and let her know what my efforts meant to you for me.

I have no choice but to continue on, not faltering now, I

am stepping way out there for Alex, myself and all the

friends whom I carry with me in life.

Before I get to sign off with writing "the end", I am going to use these last few pages to clarify a few points, and also explain why I chose to gloss over things that would have derailed my aimed purpose here.

Bare with me please, I will conclude this writing in

this way...

My father died a couple days after my birthday in May of

this year. I was still seeing Laura while living out of a car in Reading England as I shared earlier. Of course I did not go to his funeral, and yes my family hurt me with threats to join in with

Karen and her stalking efforts if I did not help them with his estate.

I told them all back in Philadelphia that I did not want anything, please just leave me alone.

Of course I am the villain to my clan because I did not come around to their wants of me to get involved with efforts distribute my father's estate.

They wanted to re-sell his house, from a reverse mortgage and that kind of stuff. I could not care one bit.

Just leave me alone I kept saying to them, I did not want their offers of money, and when that failed to bribe, then came now promises and threats to hurt me online hereafter. Just thought I should share that bit.

Oh well, I guarantee anyone reading this, how I am not in some unique situation of being saddled with a family like this.

This is what I did not want to write a huge thing about, is all I am sharing.

Here I am, 62 years old, an Orphan who is walking around with a woman's name tattooed on my back, no job, no money...just like it has been the past 4 years.

The purpose of this work cannot be a litany of lament, which then ends in a gripe, as that's not fair to me for all the many brilliant things that I still managed to pull off.

Like I said, from Podcasts, to British Television, to this new film about me and my story with Alex (or others), I have reached millions of lives with my message...with Jayne's message. Yeah, with Jayne's message of kindness.

I have so many friends in life, I am so close to going from homeless drifter, to having a stable home all the time. I know I will get there one day.

I did my utmost best in my efforts for this new project about post-release for my friend Arthur, I will continue to try for Alex and I to raise enough money to finish our film, or just have him come here and see me alive would be cool as anything.

Lastly I have really made an effort to not hurt my own daughter Lara with my detailing the unyielding actions of her mother in a slanted way. I haven't said what I could have in writing for this reason.

I am so aware of how hard it must be for a child to know, but not be allowed to love her own father, all for a sake of punishment from her mother.

I get it. I may no longer have my mother alive to promise her that I will try for her no matter what, to never let anyone steal my kindness as she'd say.

That now is my promise to you that I will go on being politely good. I have some next level ability to connect with others and I think I understand it now.

I have an awareness like some gifted artist that my voice is tormentingly beautiful, and that somehow pain of life is a honing of a my voice. It is intrinsic to suffering. Something so powerful that we all find it is alluring, and yet haunting. I'm grateful it helps me reach others in pain. I will continue to try and use this gift.

I can really fuck this all up by taking something so precious and squandering it on cheap acts, or a cheap character. I never want to be that low down with deeds.

Honestly, this is why I try so hard now to not want to be mundane in life. I want to spend each day like I am back on Death Row, to where each day felt like I was stealing something from a timed event that I was prolonging.

I want so much to leave a legacy that merits respect the ones I held myself up before in life.

Right now as I end this writing, I keep feeling still as if I am exactly where I was meant to be at this time.

I am exactly where I had to be to write this book here in 2023, to get that one last effort done now, so that the next man or woman can embrace what I have shared while,then be stronger for it.

I still have an ability with self perspective to appreciate and love myself without faltering to say this aloud.

I like my chances to do so much good in life as long as my brain holds out, and that alone makes me a winner.

For the ones I lost connections with along this journey...

Maybe if you read all of this, then we can at least come to an agreement that it is all well beyond one day, or some deed that we do in life that defines us.

I am okay with not having one enemy because I refuse to let anyone own me with hate. I hope you understand that I don't allow this in mind, you have been dismissed.

For all the ones who read this that had no idea who I was

before now, thank you for the chance let me get this all down in writing. I really am so aware that it is you who will bless me, or consider me a waste of your time. For this alone, I promise that was all I could seek from a reader as I put this out there for anyone to share.

I started off life a second time at the age 42. That is still the crazies thing which I ever typed or wrote down in my life on a piece of paper. That just never stops feeling weird.

But I have a question for anyone who gets to this point in this book:

What would you have done at age 42 and ended up in my shoes?

Seriously, I often wonder what anyone else could have done starting off where I did, and then going through exactly what I have had to face since that one point alone.

I think without boasting, that I did a really amazing effort despite so many actions of an aimed stalking, loss of money, loss of love, loss of housing... just all of it.

Yes, I am okay with how things played out despite all of those negatives.

That is what compels me to think that, since I paid full fare in every possible way for me to be here now, surely I am deserving to see what happens next to my life.

I won't kill myself, but the cloud in my head beacons me at times, and then it makes me a bit wary of how well I am handling life. I have to fight this crap in my head from a brain injury, but I still have a loving nature. That will be my focus to offset this.

I will keep using Neuroplasticicty teaching to stave off the progression of my brain injury with a determined effort is all that there is really. That's all I got. The end.

With Love always,

Nicky

Printed in Great Britain
by Amazon